# The How To Meet A Woman Collection

CASSIE LEIGH

# TITLES BY CASSIE LEIGH

## DATING FOR MEN
Online Dating for Men: The Basics
Don't Be a Douchebag
You Have a Date, Don't F It Up
The How to Meet a Woman Collection

## DATING FOR WOMEN
Online Dating for Women: The Basics
Online Dating is Hell

## DOG-RELATED
Puppy Parenting Basics
Puppy Parenting in an Apartment
Dog Park Basics

## COOKING-RELATED
You Can't Eat the Pretty

# CONTENTS

# Online Dating For Men: The Basics

CASSIE LEIGH

# CONTENTS

# INTRODUCTION

So you've decided to give online dating a try. Maybe a few of your friends found their spouses that way, or you're tired of the bar scene, or you're recently out of a long-term relationship and wouldn't even know where to go to find the bar scene, or maybe you want to tell your mom that you're making some sort of effort to meet someone without actually having to meet them.

Whatever the reason, you want to give this online dating thing a try. And, because we all hate rejection, you'd like to do it the "right way." Well, good on ya. I admire your starry-eyed optimism and resolve.

Unfortunately, you don't even know where to begin. What site should you choose? What should you say in your profile? What pictures should you use?

There are a lot of moving parts to online dating, and hopefully this book will help you with all of those questions and more.

Can you stumble through it alone? Absolutely. You can get started in online dating without spending a dime. Join a free site today and you'll be good to go within the hour.

But if you want to actually find a quality woman, it's probably a good idea to think through a few things first.

I can't promise success—no one can—but I can at least help give you a good solid start.

Online dating requires healthy amounts of persistence, optimism, and luck. But you know the saying, the harder you work, the more luck you'll see.

So let's get started and give you every advantage we can.

# DISCLAIMER:
## TARGET AUDIENCE

Before we go any further, I want to point out that this book is geared towards men. Like it or not, women's and men's online dating experiences are very different and it turns out it's a lot simpler to focus on one group or the other rather than trying to go back and forth.

Also, in this context, we're talking about heterosexual men. I, quite frankly, don't have enough insight into the LGBT experience to do it justice from a dating advice perspective. While some of the chapters will be useful to anyone entering into online dating, I think it may fall apart after that. A man dating a man is not going to have the same issues as a man dating a woman.

(And for all of you that just said or thought something like, "Amen to that," please take a moment to picture me giving you my stare of death before you continue.)

The advice in this book is based on my experience online dating in the United States. If your country has a robust online dating culture, like the U.S., then what I say here may be true for your country as well. But, having tried online dating in a smaller country with a less developed online dating culture, I can say that my experience there was very, very different than my experience in the U.S.

So keep that in mind, too. Don't blindly follow advice if it doesn't work for you.

# WHAT IS YOUR GOAL?

The first thing you have to do before anything else is determine why you're doing this. Because your reasons for online dating are going to drive every other choice you make. This is just for you. Tell your friends or mom whatever you want, but be honest with yourself. Because what you want will drive everything from your user name to the site you use to who you choose to communicate with.

Are you looking for lasting love or just trying to find someone to hook up with for a little fun?

If you're just looking for a good time, this whole online dating thing is going to be much, much simpler for you than it is for the person trying to find "the one". Not as easy as it is for a woman looking for sex, obviously, but it's still easier to find someone for a night than to find someone for a lifetime, yes?

If you want sex, you're willing to be open about it, willing to choose sites geared towards that sort of thing, and willing to hustle enough to get to yes, you'll find it.

For a one night stand you basically need someone willing to do what you want to do who doesn't repulse you so much you don't want to do it anymore. For a lifetime love you need someone you're going to like no matter what shit goes down.

Lost jobs, cross-country moves, illness, weight gain, depression, aging, dogs, kids, vacations, etc., etc.

Yeah. Pretty easy to see that the standard for one night is a lot less than the standard for a lifetime.

Now, I'm not saying you're going to end up with some hottie. If you want good looks AND sex, well, that's a much harder goal. Especially if you aren't amazingly good-looking yourself. I mean honestly, let's think this one through for a second.

Figure for every ten guys looking to just get some tonight there are two women who want the same thing. That means that each woman gets to choose from at least five possible choices, which means that you have to offer more than those other four guys. Not the time to be shooting for the stars. Let all the other guys aim for that one really hot chick who wants something casual, while you aim a little lower and actually end up with someone tonight.

Just a thought.

Of course, as someone who always advocates at least trying for the best you can get, that's a bit painful to write. You never know when that perfect ten will say yes, so might as well try.

BUT. This is online dating and so many men think that way it can get pretty painful pretty fast. I am by no means a ten, but I get enough of those might as well try messages on some of the sites to almost drive me away from online dating altogether.

So let's do this: Let's say that you will get to "yes" much faster if you're realistic about what you can offer and aim accordingly.

Enough of that digression. Back to the point.

If you just want sex with someone around your age and willing, it's pretty easy. Be honest about it and find the sites or apps that are known for that sort of thing and then work it until you get a yes. (There's a reason good salesmen usually do well with the ladies.)

If you want lifelong happiness with one special person, it's going to be much more challenging. Not impossible, just challenging.

Online dating is still dating. And a lot of the issues that kept you from finding a partner in the real world are going to keep you from finding someone online, too. But at least with online dating you can see a much larger pool of potential mates and you get to do it at home in your pajamas or when you're standing in the checkout line at the grocery store.

If you're looking for something serious, don't get discouraged. You can find a life partner through online dating. I have multiple friends who are happily married to people they met online.

Just know that finding that special person to spend the rest of your life with will be far more challenging than finding someone to spend a night with.

The men who are most successful at online dating are the ones who are persistent and don't let a few bad dates or non-responses get them down. And who maintain a positive attitude when interacting with potential matches.

Honestly, if you're looking for someone truly amazing and special and you haven't exhausted the friend-of-a-friend referrals and haven't yet approached that cute girl you see every week at rock climbing, I'd suggest doing that first before you wade into online dating. But if you've exhausted all your real world possibilities or like the idea of getting to peruse a woman's info before you take the next step, then online dating it is.

Okay, so back to the main point of the chapter:

Why are you online dating? What do you want?

Sex?

Friendship?

A fuck buddy?

A steady Friday night date that doesn't care who your Saturday night is spent with?

A long-term, but not marriage-minded, committed relationship?

Marriage?

Marriage and babies?

You can find any of the above. You just have to approach it the right way.

Step one is being honest with yourself about what you want. Step two is being honest with others about what you want. (And if you really aren't sure, like a friend of mine wasn't, choose one but be open to women that fall outside of that choice.)

# A MOMENT'S PAUSE:
## LEVEL SETTING

Whether you find someone or not will also depend very much on what you're looking for. If you want a nice, typical, sweet girl of average looks, you can probably find her. If you want an ex-model who's now an astrophysicist, well...that's going to be harder. (Just like in real life.)

Hopefully not impossible. Although, really, how many ex-model astrophysicists are out there?

I feel with men I have to emphasize more this concept of aiming to the right level because with online dating men initiate the majority of the communication. Which means you are the one that drives your online dating experience.

So while you're figuring out what you want out of this, also think about what you can realistically achieve. You will see hot women on these sites. Women that you can message, but who are so clearly wrong for you it's not even funny.

Do you approach them? It's tempting, but I'd argue that you shouldn't waste your time on those kinds of girls.

Let me give you a parallel example.

Most of us are familiar with the concept of applying for college. While it might be great to walk through life saying you went to Harvard, most people don't apply there. Why? Because they take a realistic look at their test scores, GPA, and activities and say, "No way in hell could I get in there. So why waste the time and money to apply?"

Instead they apply to schools that are in range for them whether that's the local junior college, a state school, or some lesser known but highly rated school.

Approach dating the same way. Sure, you can keep going after the Harvards of the dating world and maybe someday you'll get a yes. In the meantime, you're sleeping alone and getting older. And poorer. Because some of those girls might say yes just for the free meal. (Our society fucks up pretty women's heads...and men that want to get into their pants and buy them shit to get there make it worse.)

So focus on what you really want. And if it isn't someone to impress your friends with, aim for something lasting and realistic. Find a woman who is on your level, whatever level that is.

And if you really must go after the Harvards of the world, you better bring something to the table to attract that woman's attention, whether it's looks, money, or an amazing personality. (Or just the ability to not be a completely sex-crazed douchebag.)

Also, if you do go that way, do it with absolute confidence. Do not let her know that you think she's above you. Believe when you approach her that she'd be lucky to be with you. Your confidence may just win her over.

# PICKING A SITE OR APP:
## STEP ONE – FREE OR PAID?

Now that you know what you want from online dating, it's time to pick a site or app.

Ah, choices.

There are so many sites or apps out there and they're changing all the time, so I'm not going to recommend specific ones. I'm just going to give you some general things to think about.

First, you need to decide whether to choose a paid site (like eHarmony or Match) or a free site (like OkCupid or Plenty of Fish).

In my experience, the ones that charge money generally attract more serious users. From what I've seen, the free sites tend to have more men that are less accomplished professionally, less skilled at communicating with a woman, and generally on the younger end of things. Or recently divorced or separated and trying to save money.

Which means that for you, if you're not one of those things, you'll stand out from the crowd. Of course, if you're too much not like that you may raise the question as to whether you're real. I remember seeing a profile on one of those sites for a law firm partner who was incredibly good-looking. I have to admit that, compared to who else was on that site, I wondered if someone hadn't created a fake profile. I passed him by for that reason.

What you need to understand as a man approaching women on one of the free sites is that the signal to noise ratio is insane. Meaning, for every legitimately interesting message a woman receives, she probably receives twenty that make her consider giving this whole dating thing up and just joining a nunnery. It makes your job a lot harder. She will be much more on the defensive on a site like that.

Now, having said that, if you want casual and quick, a free site is probably the way to go. Because a girl looking for casual isn't going to mind a "Hey hawtie, what's up?" message and she'll be on there and off of there so fast that it won't matter what other crap she gets as long as she finds someone to have fun with.

If you're looking for a serious relationship or marriage, then I say spend a little money. The women who are looking for serious are much more likely to be on the paid sites. I had a friend who recently tried online dating for the first time and her choices were eHarmony and Match. She didn't even think about the free sites.

When I've done them—and I have—it's been because I felt like I should be dating, but didn't really want to put any money into the effort so I knew I could slap up a profile and feel like I was making progress without it costing me anything. Not the kind of girl you want to date.

(Having said that, I will say that a friend of mine met her husband on OkCupid. So it can happen.)

In terms of the paid sites, how long should you sign-up for? I say three months.

My male and female friends who were really serious about finding someone (which means working it hard enough to generate multiple dates per week until they found someone) generally managed to do so within ten weeks or so of joining the site.

And, honestly, even if you don't find someone within three months, you'll want to move on to a new site because, even with the bigger sites, the pickings get slim after a while.

However, many of the sites offer ridiculous price discounts if you join for longer. The last site I joined cost $11 a month if you joined for a year or $40 a month if you joined for three months. (They do this because it makes it look like they have more members than they do. It also gives them more matches to send you even if the person they're sending you hasn't been online in six months. Something my friend can attest to after she dated a guy for three months and then went back to the same site for new matches and everyone they sent her had been inactive forever.)

So, free for fun, paid for serious, and if you join a paying site, plan for three months.

# PICKING A SITE OR APP:
## STEP TWO – PRIVACY

Next you need to think about privacy. When you date in the real world, your dating life tends to stay separate from your professional life unless you deliberately let the two mix. Date your co-workers and your personal life becomes everyone's business. Get drunk with your co-workers and hook up with some random person at the bar while they're watching, that gets back to them, too. But spend your weekends at your neighborhood bar with your friends from high school and no one really cares or knows.

Online dating is different. First, some sites make your online dating profile public in order to attract other members. Is that okay for you? Are you comfortable with having your boss, co-workers, or other professional colleagues able to see your profile?

Some of these public sites ask about smoking, drug usage, sexual preference, sexual experience, etc. Would you feel comfortable answering those questions honestly knowing that anyone can see them? (If you don't answer honestly, what's the point? The people you meet on there are not going to be who you want to meet or you're not going to be who they want to meet.)

You still have to think about this with the subscription sites, too. I had a good buddy who was on Match for a long time and they kept suggesting the secretary in our office as a potential match for him. She could see everything he said about himself, which was interesting since he was not-yet divorced when he joined and the fact that he was getting divorced wasn't exactly public knowledge yet.

I once had a match that turned out to be a guy I went to high school with. Another time a site suggested a former co-worker as a potential match.

Are you comfortable having the people in your life see your dating profile? Because if you're going to date online, it will happen.

Think about it now before you have to deal with it in the office on Monday morning or at Thanksgiving with the family.

The other privacy issue you need to consider is what the site reveals about you by the way it's structured.

I don't know of any sites that use your full name, but there are some that show your real first name to other users. (eHarmony, for example.) That's fine for people with names like Jane and Mike, but not so good for people with really unique names.

I have a friend with a unique enough name that you can use her first name and the city she lives in (which most of these sites also show) to find her home address and LinkedIn profile which lists her current employment and the schools she attended.

Maybe you don't think that's an issue. You think, "So what? What if your matches can find you in the real world?" If you like a girl, you're going to tell her those things eventually, right?

Here's the thing. Just like in real life, you will meet some crazy fucking people online dating. (On some days it seems like that's all there is.) Do you really want someone you've never met showing up on your front doorstep because they can't understand why you shut down that match when you two are clearly soul mates?

No? Then think carefully about what you're revealing about

yourself and find a site that works within your comfort level.

(By the way, the way to solve this with eHarmony is to know about it when you sign up for your account and provide an initial or nickname when you list your name. As far as I know, once you put in your name it doesn't let you change it, so you have to get this right when you join.)

# PICKING A SITE OR APP: STEP THREE – COMMUNICATION PREFERENCES

Okay. So, you're going to pick a site that aligns with your goals and gives you the privacy you need. Next you need to give some thought to how you like to communicate with people.

Some options (like eHarmony) have a structured communication approach. You get to ask three multiple-choice questions, then they answer, then they ask you three multiple-choice questions. Then you get to ask three open-ended questions, then they answer, and ask you three open-ended questions, then ...You get the point.

With those sites, your first few interactions are structured. It's good for men in two ways. First, it's less painful for women to be on those sites because they're not getting bombarded with the whole "hey, hottie" kind of e-mails that some men like to send. (Not you, of course, right?)

Second, it gives you something to say when you reach out to a woman. You don't have to think about something witty to say about her profile, you just choose your three questions and hit send. She's already communicating with you by the time you have to actually form unique sentences, which gives you a little bit of "good karma" with her.

Random aside. They did this study with political signs. They'd go door-to-door and ask if they could put this little sign in the person's window. Most people said yes. It was very small and innocuous. Then they came back a few days later with a gigantic sign to put in the person's yard and asked if that was okay. Most people asked about the gigantic sign first said no. But a decent percentage of the people who had agreed to put the tiny sign in the window said yes, because they'd already agreed to display a sign previously.

Think of these structured communication sites like that. You sent your three questions and she replied. You sent three more, she replied. You sent your must haves/can't stands, she replied. You have three "yes" responses from her before you have to venture out on your own. So even if you screw up that first open communication, she'll still probably respond to you.

The other key thing about structured communication steps is that they're designed to ferret out key differences, so you can weed out bad matches early on.

There are advantages to structured communication. But it can also kill the momentum, destroy any natural chemistry that exists between two people, or mask someone's social ineptitude.

(Also, keep in mind with eHarmony that if you choose to provide your own answer, saying "all of the above" or "A and C" are useless answers, because the person reading your answer can't see what your choices were. And unless they've been doing this a lot, they don't even remember what the choices might have been.)

Back to the disadvantages of the structured approach.

Imagine meeting someone in real life. Instead of getting to just chat with them and let the conversation go where it will, you have to ask and respond to a set of structured questions that don't show your personality and don't let the other person show theirs.

*"What are your must haves?"*

*"Well, I want a man who is kind, funny, and intelligent. What are your must haves?"*

*"I want a woman who is physically passionate, fit, and kind. What are your can't stands?"*

*"I don't like men who objectify women."*

And so on and so forth.

Yawn.

If you're looking for marriage and babies, maybe the structured approach is better. It lets you address some of those key issues before you get ahead of yourself. If you're looking for tonight's hook-up, it's a definite waste of time and energy.

There are sites that don't put you through that approach, but will still have serious-minded people on them. Your best bet is to ask around.

Do an internet search or two. Not for the sites, most don't tell you enough to make that determination, but for bloggers who review the sites. See what others have to say and decide if that approach will work for you.

# STRUCTURED COMMUNICATION:
# A FEW MORE THOUGHTS

I mentioned above that one of the benefits of structured communication is that it lets you weed out bad matches. Of course, this only works if you actually pay attention to the answers.

Let me give you an example. One of my matches said he doesn't like women who watch TV. I watch a decent amount of it. Says so right there in my profile. He put it on his list of can't stands. I wrote back and pointed out that I watch a lot of it. He kept writing me.

There is no point in using structured communication that's designed to highlight key differences between you and the person you're communicating with unless you actually use it to do so.

On this particular site I tend to eliminate a decent number of matches at the must have/can't stand stage. I don't think I've ever had a man eliminate me at that stage. Not once. Don't do that. Actually read the answers. It isn't about getting through to open communication so you can ask for a date. It's about communicating. Listen to what she says. And don't be afraid to shut it down if it doesn't work.

Also, since we're digressing here. As much as appearance and sex matters to you, do not emphasize it. If a man's ten must-have traits include sexually experienced, sensual, physically demonstrative, and physically fit, I close the match down. Not because I'm anti-sex, but because the man still hasn't grown up enough to realize that there's more to a good relationship than being with a hot woman who wants to have sex with him. And that the time to discuss sex and passion is not when you're communicating online with a complete stranger.

See, men don't go through what women do. So let me try to share with you what it can be like...

From the age of fifteen onward, I had adult men very confidently and openly telling me how sexy I was. Sometimes quite explicitly. Now, when you're fifteen and just got curves, it can be pretty fun to see that men find you attractive. But fast-forward ten years and when that's still all strange men say to you it starts to get old.

That's why women become bitchy in public. Because a lifetime of "I wanta fuck you" gets old. So, let's assume that if you're online dating and the woman hasn't clearly listed religious or moral beliefs about sex, that she's into it.

Yes, I know. There are men who found themselves in sexless relationships that never want to go there again, so *it matters*. I get it. But I'm telling you that your odds of getting to the point with a woman where you have the chance for sex to happen go up if you play it a little cool and focus on other things first.

Just my personal opinion. I'm sure there are women out there who would feel very differently about this. I'm sure there are women out there who live to have strange men tell them how sexy fine they are today.

Do as you will, I'm just warning you why it may backfire on you.

# PICKING A SITE OR APP:
## STEP FOUR – LEVEL OF CONTROL

Okay, you've found a site that aligns with your goals, gives you the privacy you need, and lets you communicate in the way that works best for you.

What next?

Decide whether you want a site that will let you choose your own matches or one that's going to help you find the "right" match for you.

If you're looking for casual, you probably don't care too much about the "right" match. To be physically compatible you probably don't even have to like each other. (And now is not the time to digress into the "be careful who you sleep with because you may end up liking them so much you stay with them even though you hate a lot of things about them" lecture. Although, well, what I just said.)

If you're serious about finding a long-term relationship, it's possible that a site that chooses for you will help you get past certain biases you might have.

You know, like you only go for women who are blonde, between 5'4" and 5'6", and whose names end in –ie.

The benefits of a site that filters matches based upon your

personality profile is that theoretically you're only focusing on all those other attributes after they've found you people who are compatible on the emotional/psychological level.

Theoretically.

Now, let's stop and discuss this for a minute.

I've tried a few of these sites and, in my experience, they don't always work as well as you'd like them to. Some, like OkCupid, allow the users to decide whether to use the matching algorithms. They tell each user the percent compatibility between them and their potential match, but you can contact anyone.

In my experience men rarely if ever let a low compatibility score keep them from reaching out to a woman they find attractive. And, since answering the questions that generate the compatibility numbers is optional, most users just skip it, which means that even if it matters to you most women won't have answered enough questions for it to work.

Everyone will be 85% compatible at most because they answered a whole ten questions and only five of those overlap with the ten you bothered to answer.

What could be really helpful in narrowing down possible matches isn't at all. Which is too bad because it's the only site I know of where you can have some pretty freaky preferences and use those matching algos to find other people with the same kinks.

(If you do have some sort of specific preference, then answer the damned questions and pay attention to the answers. And be honest in your answers. I rant about this in *Don't Be A Douchebag*—a book you will hopefully never need to read.)

Some sites, like eHarmony and Chemistry, force you to complete a questionnaire before you can join and then they use the results to choose matches for you.

What about those sites?

Well, remember that whole discussion about how there are a lot of perfectly decent ordinary folks that do online dating? I think those sites work great for them.

Someone like me? Not so much.

This isn't arrogance talking (although I am arrogant), but I'm just not normal.

I've taken the Myers-Briggs (MBTI) a few times and supposedly my personality type is present in less than 5% of the population. Which, given my experience on those sites, seems pretty accurate. That means that there are a very small number of men that are good fits for me.

If those sites only gave me that handful of matches that were truly compatible, that would be fine. I'd rather have a small number of matches that really work for me than ten a day. Instead, they give me lots of matches that just don't work.

Each time I've taken one of those questionnaires, the site nailed my personality profile and what I'm looking for. I'd read it and think, "Yes, this. This is me and what I want."

And then they'd give me men that didn't meet it.

If you have a unique personality type, expect to have a lot of matches that aren't what you're looking for. And expect that just because the site tells you that someone is compatible with you, that doesn't really mean they are. In my experience, they provide matches when one side or the other will find the match interesting, not when both sides will.

(As an example, if you're a Builder-type on Chemistry, just avoid the Explorer-types. You may find them interesting, but chances are they won't feel the same way...)

What do you do if you are one of those unique personalities? Is it better to avoid the personality matching sites?

Maybe. But, problem is, there aren't going to be more people like you on the other sites. (Unless people with your personality type tend to choose the same kind of parameters so go for the same types of sites in which case just follow your gut about what you like the best.)

At least with the personality matching sites you have a snowball's chance in hell of getting a good match. On the other sites the haystack you're searching through is even bigger and the chance of finding that needle (e.g. match) are really small.

Again, this is assuming what you want is long-term. Short-term, who cares?

Bottom line? Unique personalities need to be prepared to be frustrated by a lack of appealing choices and need to force themselves to stick with it longer than normal folks.

But back to the basic question. Do you choose a site that picks matches for you or choose a site that lets you pick your own matches?

If you choose one of the sites where it's a free-for-all, you are facing more intense competition. Everyone can message that woman that interests you. On the matching sites, the woman "only" gets ten to twenty matches a day, not all of whom will message her. (Although a fairly high percentage do.) On the open sites, she gets as many messages as there are men who saw her profile and liked it that day.

So, more competition.

And, you're much more likely to focus on all the wrong criteria.

Like what? Well, you tell me.

If I gave you a site with a million women on it and told you to enter search criteria so we could narrow it down for you, what would you enter first? If you're a stereotypical guy (and, yes, there are always exceptions you special snowflake you), you'd probably start with: Age. Height. Eye color. Hair color. Body type.

Most men put a premium on physical looks. Nothing wrong with that, but it makes finding what you're looking for that much harder. If you want casual, maybe the best place to start is with someone looking for casual. If you want serious, maybe it's more important that the woman want the same things in life that you do.

Plus, at least three of the items on that list can change. I could go out tomorrow, dye my hair black, get blue contacts, and lose or gain ten pounds in the next month. Far more important to find someone mentally compatible first.

Really, it is.

Even for sex.

Maybe especially for sex.

(I'm not going to elaborate on that one, just think it through. And if you don't get it, well, hm. Maybe you're reading the wrong self-help book…)

On the free sites, there's also such a thing as choice overload.

They've done studies that basically say that having too many choices is worse than having a limited number of choices. If you can only have A, B, or C, you're pretty happy when you get B. If you can have A-Z, then you're comparing B to everything else you could have had and feel less satisfied.

Limited choices help result in long-term relationships. Or making a choice at all.

You don't want to get the "ooh shiny" syndrome and spend months on the site never getting past the first date because there was someone else who looked like maybe they were more interesting and while you were off checking that new girl out you lost the one you'd already found.

If you do go free, do it with focus. Get in, get what you want, and get out.

# AN ASIDE:
## PEOPLE LIE

You have to be careful with online dating because people lie. Many profiles are what you might call aspirational rather than realistic.

If you honestly think that searching for fit women is going to get you size 2 women and nothing else, I'd like to sell you some ocean-front property in Arizona. There might be a few in there. But there'll be a lot of size 10 women who go to the gym five times a week and think that counts. And know that "healthy" probably means slightly overweight. Because who wants to call themselves fat? That's what those other people who weigh fifty pounds more are, not me.

Also be careful of anyone whose age is listed as 29, 39, or 49. They could very well be 30, 40, or 50 and just be lying so they can appear in the lower age bracket searches.

Just like in the real world, people are insecure and most aren't comfortable with who they are. (Don't be one of those people, by the way. Just because others lie doesn't mean you should.)

Always proceed with caution. Even photos can deceive.

# PICKING A SITE OR APP: STEP FIVE – SPECIALTY SITE OR POPULAR SITE?

Alright. So, that's the basics.

One, find a site that aligns with your goals.

Two, find one that gives you the privacy you need.

Three, find one that lets you communicate in the way that works best for you.

Four, find one that provides you with the right tools to help find the person you're looking for.

What else?

What about those specialty sites? Should you use them?

Maybe. But remember that the more niche the site, the smaller the population of potential matches. Which is fine if the focus of the site matters to you enough or if that helps you narrow down your choices to a really great population of possibles. But don't assume that it'll work that way.

Let me give you an example.

I recently found an online dating site where you could post about books you liked and find other singles that liked the same books. Perfect for someone like me. I'm a voracious reader and I believe you can tell a helluva lot about someone by what they like to read.

So I checked out the site. There were a ton of men on there who had experienced life-changing transformations after reading *Outliers* by Malcolm Gladwell. Me? I hated that book. I thought the guy covered really interesting topics and then drew poor conclusions based upon unsubstantiated facts. I swore to never read another book by him, which meant I certainly had no interest in dating any man who thought it was the best book he'd ever read.

Interesting site, but obviously not for me. It didn't attract my type of guy. Which is when I realized that, as much as I love to read, most of the men I've really clicked with over the years haven't been big readers. Whatever it is that connects me to the men I like, it's not their ability to discuss the latest bestseller. As a matter of fact, there's no way to kill my mood faster than to have some guy spout off about a book I really liked, because it's rare for me to talk to someone about a book I liked or disliked and have us agree on the details of why we liked or disliked it.

Another example is a site for dog lovers. I love my dog and it would make life so much easier if I could find someone who wanted to hang out at the dog park on weekends or understands why I don't want to leave my dog alone just to go have dinner with a stranger.

But there are different types of dog lovers. I take my pup to the lake to swim and let her roll in the mud. She generally has a handful of leaves tangled in her coat on any given day. Well, a dog-lover site full of men who dressed their Shih-Tzus in pink dresses and went to dog shows wouldn't work for me.

So do your homework before you choose a specialty site. And make sure there are enough choices on there to make it worth your time. If you can, look at some actual profiles before you take the plunge.

I will say that if you're religious-minded, it's probably a very good idea to use one of the sites focused on your religion, because shared religious views help form a stable long-term relationship and most of those sites have enough users to be worthwhile. As a non-religious person, I can say that people like me will usually avoid the religious sites, so you also aren't going to find yourself really liking someone who doesn't share the same fundamental beliefs as you if you stick with one of those sites. (And, trust me, that happens and it hurts.)

# PICKING A SITE OR APP: STEP SIX – HOW MANY TO START WITH

I recommend that women just choose one site at first because the level of responses they receive is so overwhelming it just doesn't make sense to try more than one site. For men that's obviously not going to be an issue. (Because, face it, men do 90% of the reaching out on these sites.)

Men can definitely juggle more than one site. BUT. Do not lose your focus. It can be easy to send off a bunch of messages to women and then get some responses and start going back and forth and lose track of when it was you communicated with each woman last.

Me? I shut down a match after a week if I haven't heard from him. I'm not a fan of being Plan B'ed. Either you saw my profile and are interested enough to move towards meeting in person or you're not. And dropping off the face of the Earth for a week tells me you're not.

So join multiple sites if you want, but make sure you don't get in over your head.

# JUST BECAUSE SHE RESPONDS DOESN'T MEAN SHE'S INTERESTED

You're not going to like this one...

Ugly truth time. Just because you message a woman and she responds, doesn't mean she's interested in you. Sucks, doesn't it?

Why, you ask, would a woman respond if she's not interested?

A few reasons. Some nice, some not.

She's new to this and feels like she should give every guy a chance.

She's too polite not to respond. It feels rude to ignore you, but she doesn't know how to say that she's not interested so she responds hoping you'll just go away.

She's been told she's too picky, so she's trying really, really hard not to be. Even though you're not her physical type and you said that nasty thing about all women being too emotional (do not say things like that when trying to attract women...) she's going to give it a few messages before she shuts you down.

She likes the attention. She has a profile up to see just how many men message her and gets a thrill from it.

She's on there not to meet someone for real, but to get a free night out. (Those women exist, but don't go into this thinking all women are like that or you will find that your negativity drives off the women who aren't like that.)

It was Tuesday and she responds to all men who message her on Tuesday. (Yeah, that's me being a smartass. Sometimes people just respond for no reason whatsoever.)

The key here is to know that just because you messaged a woman and she responded, that doesn't mean anything. The whole point of this is to take it to the real world, so until you meet in person, you don't have anything real to talk about. (And, even then, you may not because she may just be being polite or really, really trying to be open-minded.)

# ANOTHER THOUGHT

I sometimes find it creepy to see that men are checking out my profile. Especially if they do it too often or when I'm online. One of the sites does pop-up boxes in the corner for every guy looking at your profile. I've logged on to respond to messages and had them pile on top of each other in the corner like some sort of zombie attack.

You don't want to be part of that. You especially don't want to be the guy that sees she's online, checks out her photo, and shoots off a message. (Unless this is about sex, in which case it all works differently.)

On the free sites you can get around notifying a woman that you checked out her profile by looking for matches when you're not logged into the site. Do all your match searches anonymously and write down the user names of the women you liked, then log in and message them.

And, unless you're looking for casual, don't message a woman while she's online. You're not the only one doing it and it puts you in a class of guys you don't want to be associated with.

# TIME TO TAKE A BREATHER AND SUMMARIZE

There's a lot to consider, but you probably aren't going to go wrong if you stick with the big sites.

Honestly, if it's too much to think about, just try Match your first time out of the gate. It's the all-purpose site with enough members for everyone and a couple of my guy friends have had solid success on there. Not marriage, but long-term dating as well as hook-ups.

If you want casual, I hear Tinder or AdultFriendFinder work well. I would also put OkCupid or Plenty of Fish in that category.

For serious I would say eHarmony and, although I've never used them since I lack strong religious beliefs, Christian Mingle or JDate.

With all sites, here are the key things to keep in mind:

1. Pick a site that aligns with what you want. Free is more likely to be casual, paid is more likely to be serious.

2. Pick a site that meets your privacy needs while realizing that you probably cannot maintain your privacy completely.

3. Only pick a specialty site if you're really, truly passionate about that particular niche and you can see that the type of people on that site are passionate about it in the same way you are.

4. Choose a site that matches how you like to communicate.

5. Choose a site that will give you the right tools to meet someone and, if you have a unique personality type, be prepared for any personality matching algorithms to not be as effective for you as they are for others.

6. Do your homework. Ask friends what worked for them. Find out how a site works before you join it.

7. Remember that people lie and don't assume that they really meet your criteria just because their profile says they do.

That's about it for finding a site. Next, what to do once you find one.

# PICKING A USER NAME

Now that you've found a site, you need to think about how you're going to present yourself.

Not every site requires user names, but a lot of them do. And John1972 is going to get a much different response than BBoyBlitz or Lawman.

So, who are you? And how do you want potential matches to see you?

Personally, I think the name with year of birth thing is boring and shows a lack of originality. Honestly, you couldn't think of anything more creative than your name and birth year?

Also, think long and hard before you choose some sort of name like BBoyBlitz. Does that represent who you are right now? Or is that who you were ten years ago? And is the type of woman you're looking for right now the type of woman that will find a guy like that attractive?

Another thing to consider: It's fine to use a name that has some sort of hidden meaning or reference. You know, like WinterIsComing. But if you do that and a woman gets the reference, don't be a schmuck about it and say, "Wow, I didn't think a woman would get that." Then why did you use it on a dating website?

You are dating. Focus on that fact and choose accordingly.

Your user name is one of the many ways you get to market yourself. Use it well.

Another thought. Be careful about using the same user name on your dating profile as you use elsewhere. I had a match at one point who had used the same very unique user name across the Internet. I did a Google search, as you do, and found a number of interesting things he'd said elsewhere that were not at all apparent from his dating profile. Things that made me decide maybe it was time to move on.

Pick a name that you can live with, that showcases your personality, that isn't boring, and that you don't use elsewhere.

Also, stay away from the sexual references unless you're looking for casual or it really does exemplify your personality. ILuvBoobies may make your friends laugh, but will it make the type of woman you're looking for laugh? If no, ditch it. If yes, more power to you.

Always think about your goals in doing this and act accordingly.

Finally, if you are on a website that uses real names, like eHarmony, and you have a unique name then consider listing an initial, nickname, or more common abbreviation of your name that won't be so easy to Google.

# PICKING YOUR PROFILE PHOTOS

The next step is to pick your profile photos. This isn't as important for men—you can get away with crappy photos and a woman will still give you a chance—but the better your photos, the better your chances.

Do post a photo. I had a situation the first time I tried online dating where the guy didn't have a photo. I went along with it. I got burned in the end. I will never again communicate with a guy who doesn't have a photo posted.

According to OkCupid, the best photos for guys are ones where they aren't looking at the camera and aren't smiling. And there have been studies that women prefer men who look intense instead of friendly.

However, personally, I like to see a photo of a guy who looks like he'll be nice. So I prefer someone making eye contact with the camera and smiling.

Then again, I wasn't a big fan of *Fifty Shades of Grey* and it seems 90% of women were, so take that how you will.

Whatever you do, I'd avoid professionally-taken photos. You know, the kind with the blue patterned background and soft lighting. Those shots stick out like a sore thumb.

And try to post photos from different times and places. Only posting photos of you in one outfit and five poses makes me wonder what you're hiding. Did you just lose two hundred pounds? Did you used to be a woman? Why do you have no other photos of yourself?

Variety is good.

Now, if you want something more serious and long-term, then you need to think long and hard before posting too many "fun" photos of yourself. If you want a woman to see you as a provider and father of her children, you probably don't want to post a photo of yourself double-fisting shots at a frat party.

And be careful including alcohol in your photos at all. One photo with alcohol is fine. Every photo with alcohol implies that you might have a drinking problem.

You also need to think about the type of person you're trying to attract. If you want someone active and outdoorsy, then post active and outdoorsy photos of yourself. If you want someone who goes to wine tastings and art exhibits, then post photos of yourself in more sophisticated outfits or settings— wearing a suit, for example.

Also be sure the photos you're posting represent who you really are. Don't post that one photo of you doing that one really adventurous thing five years ago if you never actually do adventurous things.

My prime example of this—and maybe it's just because I used to skydive—is the guy who posts a photo of himself walking back from the landing zone after a skydive. He can't post the one of him in the air, because it was a tandem and he was just meat strapped to the front of the guy actually doing the skydive, so he posts the photo from the field. Look, it's pretty cool to have even done a tandem, but if that's all you've ever done, you were a spectator for one day. It's not you. Don't post it to pretend to be cool.

And no matter how good that photo of you with your ex was, don't use it. It's obvious when you're all dressed up and you cut off half of the photo that you must be posting a photo with an ex.

Also be careful of photos of you and one woman. If you decide to use one of those, be very clear in the photo description who that woman is. And then step back and figure out how creepy it is for you to post a photo of yourself with that woman on your dating profile.

(I had a match post about four photos of himself with his sister. It was just odd to me. I didn't write him off because of it, but it did make me pause and was a strike against him. Know you're being judged and plan accordingly.)

The other issue with having other women in your photos is that you might be conveying to your potential matches the type of women you associate with and she may not like it. I know, that's vague. Let me try to clarify.

A friend of mine had an interesting match. But all of the photos in his profile showed women in their 40's who were trying to look like they were still in their 20's. (You know what I'm talking about.) My friend is not that type. She cares about her appearance, but she's not heavy with the makeup or insane with the hair and the last time she wore a short, tight dress that showed everything was...never. So this guy got the axe, because it was clear to my friend that she wasn't going to like his friends at all.

Early on, just present yourself if you can.

I would also avoid group shots. I know, it makes you look social, so there's an argument for including them. But sometimes it comes off looking too party-like, which tips things back into the "just having a good time" category. Also, the other people in that photo don't necessarily need their photo up on a dating site.

And, if that's all you post, your potential matches may not even know which one is you. If you do post a group shot, DO NOT make it your primary photo. I have a match right now that did that and I've yet to click on his profile to see if I can even figure out which of the five people in the thumbnail photo are him.

You also run the risk that the woman looking at your photo finds one of your friends more attractive. I know that's happened with me a few times. I look at a match's photos and see a photo of him with his buddies and think, "Bummer that guy wasn't my match." Best to avoid that moment.

You want to draw someone in to you. You want them to get your communication, or that e-mail suggesting new matches, see your profile photo, and think, "He's cute..." or "Wow. He's pretty hot..."

You don't want them to be confused or distracted.

Your photos should also be current. Nothing more than a year or two old. I know, I know, you looked so good ten years ago at your best friend's wedding. But they're not going to date the you of ten years ago. They're dating who you are right now, so show them what they're getting.

Nothing worse than showing up for a date and being severely disappointed by what you find because the person lied. (Much better to show up and be pleasantly surprised.)

And, this should go without saying, post photos of yourself, not someone else. (I had a date tell me some woman used photos of her sister. WTF? What is someone hoping to achieve by doing that? You do want to meet this person in real life, right? Well, think that through...)

You should also think about the quality of the photos you post. Personally, I think professionally-taken photos stand out like a sore thumb, but the nicer the photo, the better you look. So think about using a high-resolution camera instead of a crappy phone, avoid harsh lighting, and make sure you're the focus of the photo. (There's another OkCupid blog that discusses this in far more detail.)

Here's what I recommend whether you're looking for casual or serious:

1.  Your main photo should be a close-up shot of your face.

2.  It should be a smiling photo, making eye contact with the camera, and looking friendly and open to a conversation. OR, if you want to go with OkCupid's advice, it should be a serious photo looking away from the camera. (Show that strong, manly jaw...)

3.  You should have more than one photo posted and at least one should be a full body shot. (This isn't as important for men as for women, but let a girl see what she's getting.)

4. Current photos only unless you make it clear that it's an older photo and it's up there to prompt conversation. (Like that trip you took to Tibet ten years ago.)

5. If you're going to break from the above, make sure you're doing something to trigger people's interest so they'll communicate with you.

6. Post photos that will appeal to the type of person you're looking to meet. (And that legitimately reflect your interests. If you want someone outdoorsy, you should probably be outdoorsy, too.)

7. Post quality photos taken under good lighting with a good camera and where you're the focus of attention.

# FILLING OUT YOUR PROFILE:
## PART ONE – WHAT TO SAY

Alright, so you have a site and photos. Now it's time to say something about yourself.

Let's eliminate the easy one first. If you want something casual, then you don't need to say much. Hell, you're a guy, you're going to be the one reaching out to the women, you may not need to say anything at all. Just have a good photo and pick the right kind of girl.

(What is the right kind of girl? Lots of selfies, fish lips, boob shots, group photos with lots of alcohol and large groups of partiers, and says she likes to have fun.)

For those who want something serious, it's a little trickier.

DO NOT make any statements about women as a group.

Let me give you an example. eHarmony now has this thing where they ask you questions and then they tell your match how many you agreed or disagreed on. One of those questions is, "Do you think women are too emotional?" It doesn't say some women, it implies all women. And there are men, looking to date women, that answer this question, "Yes."

Think about that for a second. You don't know me. You want to date me. And you've just told me that you think all women are too emotional. My reaction? You can kiss my ass. Next.

And, yes, ironically, that may be the reaction of a woman who is too emotional. But, as you should know, insulting women as a whole is generally not the most successful dating strategy.

Be careful in whatever you say or whatever you answer that you aren't giving women a reason to move on to the next guy. Because there is a next guy.

Harsh truth of online dating: Women get approached multiple times per day. Men have to do most of the approaching. For men, it's a bit like preparing for a job interview. Put your best foot forward.

(And this may change as you get older. My grandma says competition for the remaining single, breathing men when you're over sixty is something fierce. Women swarm these guys when they show up at her widower's group. But unless you're already there, you have to make the good impression for now.)

So no negativity towards women, okay?

Include things that will spark conversation. And try to be unique about it. Saying you watch football each Sunday, while true, isn't going to make you stand out from the crowd. Saying you play jai alai on the weekends will.

Try to mention whatever you like that isn't what everyone else and their mother likes.

And I think demonstrating a sense of humor is always a good thing. Women love men who can make them laugh.

I've seen some people advise that you don't put too much text, but I say be yourself. If you like to put a lot of text in your profile, put a lot of text. But don't feel like you have to. Short and sweet will work, too.

(Oh, and spell check and grammar check while you're at it, please.)

And, remember, privacy. Don't put things in your profile that will let someone track you down in real life. Be generic rather than specific. I wouldn't post a photo of your home or talk about where you like to go hiking. Protect yourself for now. This is more of an issue for women, I think, but men can be stalked too.

Also, watch the bragging. With the photos and with the text. That may work for a certain type of girl, but it can come off as desperately insecure to others. If you're entire profile is "I make money, see? Here's my boat and my house and my fancy car and my..." you're either shallow and have nothing else to offer or you don't realize that women want more than that.

Quiet confidence is good. Desperate showmanship, bad.

# FILLING OUT YOUR PROFILE:
# PART TWO – CATEGORIZING YOURSELF

All sites want to categorize their users. Some of those choices make a lot of sense. Are you male or female? Are you looking for someone who is male or female? Those types of questions are necessary and easy to answer for 99% of the population.

But most sites go past that. What is your religion? What is your ethnicity? What is your income? What is your education? What is your star sign?

Not only that, but how do you want your potential mate to answer those questions? And how important is it that they answer that way?

Not so easy anymore is it?

Well, let's talk about a few of those.

## RELIGION

This is a very easy question to answer if you have a clear-cut religious belief. One of my very good friends is Jewish and there was no doubt in her mind when she went looking for a husband that he needed to be Jewish as well. A good friend of my brother's is also Jewish. He ended up marrying a non-religious woman from Taiwan who converted to Judaism to please the parents. I recently went on a date with a guy who listed himself as spiritual but not religious even though he grew up Jewish.

For someone like my friend, filling out those questions is easy. You say you're Jewish and that you want someone who is also Jewish. (Or, better yet, if you're like my friend, put all of your mother's and grandmother's friends to work rooting out every single Jewish woman they know and skip online dating altogether.)

For someone like my brother's friend or the guy I dated, it's more complicated. If you're religious but not strongly enough to care whether your partner is, or strongly enough for it to impact your lives together, do you list it? It matters to some, it doesn't matter to others. If you list yourself as a certain religion and then end up with matches who were looking for that religion, are they going to be disappointed by your level of observance?

I was raised Christian, but only go to church for weddings and funerals (and try to avoid both as much as possible), but I'm also not a fan of people who are openly atheist because I think it's a bit arrogant to assume that you can firmly conclude that there isn't a higher power. But I'm also not spiritual in the sense that I feel there's some spiritual energy connecting all of us. So for me, there's never a good category to choose.

What am I? Other? Not religious? Spiritual? What I end up picking depends on my mood at the time.

And I keep that in mind when I'm setting parameters for what type of mate I'd be willing to accept. There might be a not-very-Christian man who chooses Christian who could be my perfect match. Or maybe it's the spiritual but not religious guy. The wider the net you cast, the more choices you get. But the more mismatches as well.

If you do choose certain religions as acceptable and you aren't that religious, be alert to signs that the other person is very much a believer in the religion they've listed and be clear as soon as possible that you are not.

## ETHNICITY

This is another fun one. I tend to approach this one from the "what do people see" perspective. Look at my photo and you see a white woman. You don't think mixed or multi-ethnic, you just think white. Truth of the matter is I have all sorts of different ethnic groups flowing through my veins. But I don't think that's what potential mates care about. I think they care about the woman they'll be seeing every day and introducing to their friends and family.

I also think they care about background and cultural traditions. My upbringing was also very white. Sure, we had more Christmas dinners that were Mexican food instead of ham or whatever it is normal white people have for Christmas, but all in all my upbringing was standard white-person upbringing.

So that's what I choose. And then I keep an eye out for someone who really, really wanted someone white. In the areas where I've lived, that's never been an actual issue, but it could be, so be aware of what the person you're with says.

In terms of who you want as a match, well, that's up to you. I had a friend who threw the net very wide and was open to any ethnicity. She really hit it off with a guy who was from a very different ethnic background than her. Seemed to work. Except when she thought long-term. Then she wondered what would happen when they had kids because they wouldn't look like her.

Gut check moment. I'm sure one or two people reading that just flinched. But it's a valid issue for some people and you need to know if it's one for you.

Now, maybe my friend would've grown past that little moment of whatever you want to call it. But I think it's better to think these things through before someone's heart is on the line.

Ask yourself: Would I be comfortable being seen in public as part of a couple with someone of this ethnicity? Would I be comfortable introducing someone of this ethnicity to my family? To my friends? Would I be comfortable having a child that was half this ethnicity? How would my family react to my dating someone of this ethnicity?

Ugly questions to ask yourself in this PC world of ours, but valid ones. Many people are fine being friends with members of different ethnic groups. But marrying someone of a different ethnicity? Well, not everyone is there yet. If you're not, don't waste your time or the other person's by pretending that you are.

And if you're part of an ethnic group, ask yourself if you want to run into that shit. Sure, you may be open to dating anyone, but do you really want to help that person work through all the hidden landmines they don't even know exist in their world until they start dating you?

## AGE RANGE

Men are the funniest on this one. I've seen multiple men that list the age range they're looking for as anywhere from two years younger to twenty years younger than them. Haha. You wish. I mean, sure, some men can pull this off. But are you really, truly saying that you can't stand the thought of dating a woman your own age?

I'll tell you, even when I'm in the acceptable age range for a guy like that, I tend to blow him off. Do as you will. If it's that important to you that you date younger, then do so, but I would encourage you to take any age range you think is acceptable and expand it just a bit.

Personally, I'm far more accomplished than most men my age, so I find it difficult to view younger men as equals that I would want to date. But I have to leave room for the possibility that there will be that exception to the rule, so I allow matches as much as eight years younger.

And be honest about your own age. Please. And, no, explaining that you lied about it in the profile is not being honest about it. I know, it's tough, but it is what it is and you don't want to start a relationship off with lies. At a bar you can just not answer the question. Online it's mandatory and one of the first facts that the sites provide about you.

Another thing to consider is that your age is about more than your appearance. It's about your cultural references—I grew up on G.I. Joe and Strawberry Shortcake. A girl five to ten years younger than me probably didn't. And it's about where you are in life. If you're forty-five, that is a different place than thirty-five. It's not quite the cliff it is for women, but there are some major mental adjustments men go through when they hit that big 4-0.

Just be honest about it. Seriously.

## INCOME

I don't know why any site asks this question. I find it offensive. And one I just joined doesn't even let you refuse to answer.

I expect the temptation is quite high for men to lie about this. In our society your value and worth as a man is often tied to your ability to earn money, so who wants to choose the low range, right?

But be honest about it. You think a woman won't be able to tell if you lied, but I can tell when I'm out with a guy who doesn't make as much as me. So can my friends. I had a friend recently date a guy for a few months and she knew she probably earned twice what he did even though they never told each other what they made. It was obvious from where he lived, what he drove, how he talked about money, what he wore, etc., etc.

What to list? For most people, this will be easy. You have a salary and maybe a bonus and they come out to around $X every year. For someone who is self-employed like myself, it's a helluva lot harder. The income I earned this year is five times the income I earned last year and half the income I earned five years ago. And next year, unless I change something in my current plan, I may earn next to nothing.

What number should someone like me choose? I went with the number most representative of my professional experience and place in life. A number that I have earned and that is comparable to what I would earn if I accepted a salaried position tomorrow.

I could've gone higher, but it would've been a stretch to do so. I would encourage you to choose an honest number that is in line with what you have earned and may earn again and to tip towards a higher number if you're right on the edge of a range.

## EDUCATION

This one's very straight-forward in terms of what you list. Either you have a degree or you don't. (And three credits shy of a degree is not having a degree. Honestly, if I were looking for a match I'd be far more judgmental of the person who stopped three credits shy of graduating but put down that they had a degree than I would be of the person who never went.)

If you're tempted to weigh this one heavily in terms of finding matches, ask yourself, why does her education matter to you? Do you see it as a proxy for achievement, because it's not.

I say ignore education. Unless, of course, you come from one of those families or social groups where people have to have certain credentials in order to be accepted. If that's the case, I think you should skip online dating and use friends-of-friends or a matchmaker to meet someone because those groups look for far more than just the degree.

## STAR SIGN

Should you use bizarre criteria to look for a mate? You know, like star sign?

I'm a rational, practical person and that side of my personality says, "Hell, no." But I have this great book that tells you how compatible you are with someone based upon the week of your birth and the week of their birth, and it has yet to be wrong.

So, do as you will, but if some girl comes along and you feel "it" don't pass her by just because she's a Gemini.

# TIME TO COMMUNICATE

You're ready to go. You've posted the photos and completed your profile. Time to let 'er rip.

This is when being a guy sucks. Because chances are, unless you are really, really lucky or really, really amazingly attractive, you're going to have to do all the heavy lifting. You'll have to look at profiles for potential matches and reach out to them.

Which leads men to do a few stupid things. (Do not do them.)

Like the one-liner. The "Hey, what's up?" or "How you doin'?" Now, this could work if all you want is a casual hook-up. Message enough of the right kind of girl and you'll get a response. But if you want serious? (And by serious I mean more than one date…) Skip the one-liner. Especially on the free sites. It happens to women so often it doesn't matter how amazing you are, she will blow right past that message and move on.

Another stupid one is the copy and paste. This one takes a little more effort, but is still a no go. You think to yourself, "I don't want to have to write a new message for every single woman. It's all the same crap anyway. I'll just write one message and send it to every girl." And you do. "Hi, I'm John. I'm 35 and looking for a woman who likes long walks and romantic dinners. Is that you?"

I've seen copy and paste messages that were three or four paragraphs long. Don't do this. If you must use one, at least personalize it. But the fact of the matter is that almost every single copy and paste message comes off as stilted. Because it isn't part of a dialogue. You didn't read her profile, react to it, and respond. She said something, you ignored it, and you said something else that you could've said to any of twenty people.

It doesn't work well. It also doesn't work because if she does respond to that first message, chances are your follow-up response will be so out of synch with the first message that it'll be completely obvious at that point that you were just shooting off as many first messages as you could.

Again, I think the job application analogy works here. This is you sending in your résumé. You are better off applying for a smaller number of jobs (contacting fewer women), but tailoring your résumé to each of them (sending personal messages) than you are mass-mailing one standard cover letter and résumé (the copy and paste message to every woman who looks even close to interesting.)

Focus your efforts.

So if you do skip the one-liner and the copy and paste, what should you say?

It doesn't have to be much. Pick something in her pictures or her profile that interests you and comment on it. And then ask a question. "I see you like to watch *Peaky Blinders*. That is so cool. I didn't know anyone else out there watched that show, too. Who's your favorite character?"

Done.

You've told her you saw her profile, that you read it, that she in particular interested you, and you've given her something to respond to.

Keep asking questions with every response you send her. Always give her something she needs to respond to. It's playing on her sense of politeness. You can blow off a message where someone says, "Nice picture." It's much harder to do when they say, "Nice picture. Where was that taken?"

Always ask a question. Always make it personal.

# WHO TO CONTACT

Ah, the million-dollar question. I wish I could keep men from looking at profile pictures before they decide who to contact.

Why? Because men are blinded by beauty. Maybe not all men, but a very high number. And I have seen my guys friends put themselves through more torture and suffering because of this…

But you're going to look, aren't you? Fine. Try to be a little open to women who don't fit your ideal. Hair color? Can change. Eye color? Can change. (Not as often, but it can.) Weight? Will change unless this is just a short-term thing. Especially if you go the marriage and babies route.

So look past the picture. And please read the profile. I know, that's a lot of time and effort to put in if the woman has a lot of text in her profile. But it's worth it. Because if you smoke and she says, "No smokers," you're better off moving on now. Or no drugs. Or no cats. Please. Some things really are not negotiable.

Whatever she listed in her profile was important enough for her to risk receiving fewer matches because it matters to her. So respect that and move on if you aren't what she's looking for.

Otherwise, look for women who are interesting to you. And keep in mind that if there's a huge disconnect between who you are and who she is, that's probably not going to work. I like to hike and get outside, but I'm not Miss Fitness. And yet I get messages from marathoners who like to ski and go to the gym six days a week and want a fit woman. I list my hobbies as watching TV, why are these guys messaging me?

It all comes back to the photo. Don't do that to yourself or her, okay? You'll find someone you really want to be with a helluva lot sooner if you focus on what she's saying and put less weight on what she looks like.

One more thought. Try not to judge a woman for her photos. I saw some article recently where a guy made a nasty comment about women who post a photo they took of themselves in the bathroom mirror. You know, along the lines of, "Don't you have any friends?" Think about it this way: That woman isn't polished at doing this. She's new to online dating and won't be as jaded as some other women.

As a matter of fact, she may be your best possible match right now. Think about it...

# WHAT IF YOU DON'T GET RESPONSES

First, did you listen to me about avoiding the one-liners, copy and paste messages, and personalizing what you say? Did you also listen about not focusing on the photo? If every woman you message is a '10+', you have a lot of competition and she may not have the time to respond to you because you just can't compete with the other guys she's hearing from.

When I join a new site, I get around twenty messages in that first day. I've heard of women getting up to sixty. If you are going after a woman every man is going to want you better have great photos and an amazing first message to stand out from the crowd. (Let's think the job application analogy again. What do you bring to the table that makes you worth the interview?)

Have a trusted female friend look at your photos. I had one guy who messaged me and his photos were horrible. He looked pissed off and angry in each one. And I think they were all selfies, too. My brother is one of those guys who never smiles in a photo, so I get it. You don't have to smile, just don't look like a death row inmate.

In fact, you may need to take pictures just for your dating profile. If so, do it. Grab a beer, a good camera, a few changes of clothes, and have a good friend snap some realistic photos of you relaxed and enjoying yourself. Go for a hike if you need outdoorsy photos. Whatever it takes.

I'm convinced that pretty much anyone can take a flattering photo. It's just a question of how many bad photos you have to take before you get a good one. When I was eighteen, I swear nine out of ten photos I took looked great. (Especially since that was in the film camera days and you only had so many chances to take a photo.) Now? Maybe one in forty looks good (thank God for digital cameras), but I can still get a good photo if I take enough of them. You can, too.

If you don't have any good photos and don't want to ask a friend, sit down with a remote control and a video camera that lets you take photos and shoot a couple hundred of them. (That's how I got my blog photo.)

Seriously. Do it. Women are more forgiving about looks than men, but they'll still respond better to an attractive man than an unattractive one.

If you're not getting responses also make sure that your profile, user name, and photos are in synch. I had a guy message me with a user name about rapping, photos of him hangin' in the club, and a profile that talked about how he was a real estate developer. It didn't fit. It didn't make sense. The profile interested me, but the photo and user name turned me away.

Here's the thing: Women generally have enough choices that they can be picky. They're looking for reasons to say no, not yes, to get things down to a manageable level. Remove reasons for them to walk away.

If that doesn't fix it, then it's time to think outside the box.

Be quirky. Be unique. Be bold. Be memorable.

Stand out from the crowd.

Everyone on these sites is trying to present themselves in the most flattering light, so what can you say that's real and genuine and will make a woman stop and give you a shot?

If you're not getting responses, what do you have to lose? Try it. If nothing else, you'll show confidence and that's a very attractive quality to most women.

(Note: I did not say arrogance, I said confidence.)

# SHE RESPONDED: WHAT NOW?

Well, time to write back.

We talked about this a bit above, but we'll go over it again.

What should you think about when you respond?

First, be yourself. I know the world of online dating is full of people who aren't being themselves, but if you want something real out of this, you need to be who you are from the start. Do you really want to fake who you are for the rest of your life? No. So don't do it now.

Be who you are. If a weird *Supernatural* reference pops into your head, include it. If you want to quote the latest Pitbull song, do so. Want to reference Debussy? Do it.

Second, remember that you're courting someone. I know, old-fashioned term, but good concept. You want to impress her enough that she's willing to meet you in real life. Don't insult her (unless you can do so in a flirting way). Don't argue with her. Don't correct her.

Keep your messages focused on getting to know her and letting her get to know you.

Don't complain to her about your life. Be positive.

Think back to your best dates or most memorable conversations. What were those like? Fun, interesting, engaging? Do that.

Next thing you need to understand is that you probably aren't going to have a 100% success rate. One reply does not equal a date. It equals a "didn't yet find a reason to say no." So keep that in mind. Until you get to the second date, you're still in that "looking for a reason to say no" category.

If a woman doesn't reply to your next message, that's okay. Just move on. Don't take it personal. She could've found someone else. She could've reacted to something you said that has everything to do with her and nothing to do with you.

It doesn't matter. She wasn't the one. Next.

What else should you do? As I said above, give her a reason to write back. Ask questions.

Be complimentary (but not overly complimentary). Try to focus your positive comments on what she's done or who she is, not what she looks like.

Share similar experiences if you have them.

Find common interests.

Now is not the time to figure out if she'd be willing to stay home and raise your babies. Make sure you like her first. And that she likes you.

And remember that you're still strangers to each other. Don't get too comfy. Don't start acting like you've been together for months.

What does that mean? Don't talk to her about cuddling on the couch together. Or about how you had to soak in the tub for an hour because you hurt your shoulder over the weekend.

Keep it appealing and remember that you're still getting to know each other.

Also, still protect your privacy. Don't tell her that you work at the Merrill Lynch office on H Street. Tell her you work downtown and are in financial services. You don't need her being able to find you in the real world.

Now, while you're communicating, you also need to be assessing this girl for more than just "are we compatible." You need to be looking for red flags that she is someone you need to avoid. Like what? Well...

# RED FLAGS TO WATCH OUT FOR

What do I mean by red flags that a girl is someone to avoid? I'm sure you'll come up with a few that I can't because I haven't been there myself, but let's see...

## 1. DRAMA

You've only exchanged three messages and she's already had a mini-meltdown on you about something minor. Or she told you about this one time when she was at the store and someone wouldn't serve her and she threw a drink in their face. Or...

You know this girl. We all know this girl. She's not worth it. You might like the ups and downs, but really, best avoided. Casual or otherwise. You can do better.

## 2. SHE HAS ADDICTION OR DEPRESSION ISSUES

This one's trickier. I, personally, try to avoid dates who have or have had addiction or depression issues. I don't think it's something you get over. I think it's something you manage to handle, but that means that you are never truly free of it.

Now, there are many wonderful people in this world who have overcome addictions or depression and are living perfectly happy, healthy lives. (My father was one.) There are also many people who have relapsed.

I want someone who can hold it together when the shit goes down—when we both lose our jobs and they're going to foreclose on the house and his mother is in the hospital and my brother is in a car accident. When that happens I want a guy who can keep it together and get through it, not someone who is quite likely to be facing the temptation to drink again or who spirals into a deep depression so I have to deal with him as well as everything else that's going wrong.

The hardest ones to spot are the ones that have a problem, but don't yet realize it. Where do you draw the line between someone who likes to go out and have fun and someone who has a drinking problem? Hard to tell sometimes. But if your gut tells you there's something wrong, trust it and move on.

## 3. SHE'S NOT WHAT SHE SEEMS.

Beware the woman who seems too good to be true. If you're asking yourself, "how could I possibly be lucky enough to have attracted this woman?" proceed with extreme caution and make sure to meet her in person as soon as you possibly can. She may very well be a guy named Boris who lives in the Ukraine and wants to borrow some money from you.

Keep an eye out and don't trust everything anyone tells you until you've seen it for yourself.

You aren't dating your cousin's best friend here. You're meeting someone with no connection to you or your family or friends. They could be anyone. So just play it a little cool.

And don't agree to reship an unopened package for them or to loan them money.

# CHECKING FOR COMPATIBILITY

I covered it a bit above and I'll cover it again even though you may still not listen to me.

It isn't all about the picture. Just because she's attractive doesn't mean she's a good fit for you.

Look past the pretty pictures and ask yourself if this woman is someone you could spend a significant amount of time with. I had a buddy meet some woman online dating who he absolutely detested. They dated for six months. Why? Because she slept with him and it was pretty good and he liked having sex.

I think most men have done that at one point in their lives. It happens, but really, don't go there.

Why? Because while he was in that six-month relationship it's possible that a great woman who would've also slept with him came and went and he missed her. Fast-forward ten years and he's still single and looking and those six months aren't exactly a fond memory.

Ask yourself: Will this woman make my life better? Will I be happier if I'm with her?

If the answer is no, then move on to the next woman. It is possible to find someone who is both attractive and likeable.

And if all you care about is that a woman is good-looking and you don't want anything deeper or more meaningful, fine.

That can work. There are women out there that want something as limited in their relationship. (Usually the arrangement is money for looks.) Those women are out there and it can make a great long-term partnership if you both want the same thing.

But if you find a woman who wants a man who's compatible on all levels and will accept and love her no matter what happens in the future and you know you'd dump her if she gains twenty pounds, you'll eventually destroy her and that's just not a nice thing to do to someone else. Move on.

Remember, even though this is online, you're still dealing with a human being on the other end of that computer.

Back to the point: Look past the photos and figure out if there's any real compatibility there or not.

# COMMUNICATING AWAY FROM THE SITE

Messaging back and forth on the various sites is pretty easy. It's like any conversation, except via website.

But I know some men like to communicate via e-mail or want to talk on the phone—especially on the paid sites. That can be tricky. You're asking someone to let you into their life. Do it too soon and they're liable to blow you off.

Spend too much time e-mailing and texting and talking on the phone before meeting in person and they're likely to lose interest.

The nice thing about using an online dating site is that you can message with someone, decide you're not interested, and just end the conversation without having to deal with any sort of awkward follow-up e-mails, phone calls, or texts.

If you take things to your personal e-mail account or give out your phone number, you may have to deal with that fallout. Do you want some chick texting you five times a day because you blew her off?

If you are going to give out an e-mail address, think about setting up a new one just for dating. A friend of mine gave her e-mail to some guy and he friended her on Facebook before they'd ever even gone on a date because he used her e-mail to find her account.

So not cool.

Don't do that.

As with all of this, find where you're comfortable. Just remember that these sites are set up, in part, to provide you with a safe environment to meet someone. If you step outside of that environment, you are taking on additional risk. You have to if you really want to meet someone, just be smart about it.

# SHUTTING A MATCH DOWN

Sometimes you'll communicate with a girl who seems promising, but it never seems to come together. She may be your most attractive match or your most interesting one or the only one of the bunch that likes karaoke. Whatever it is, you really like her.

But when you try to suggest getting together, she blows you off. Some of this may just be your level of comfort versus hers. But if it keeps happening, you have to question whether it's worth your time to keep going.

Me? I hate talking on the phone or texting and usually use Skype with the camera turned off, so some guy who suggested that would probably be ignored. Or I'd come back with the suggestion to just get together.

So, before you give up, try suggesting something different. If you suggested getting together and she wasn't keen, see if you guys can chat on the phone. If you suggested the phone and she didn't want to, just ask to get together.

Try to move it forward. If you can't, move on.

What if she's one of those that disappears for days at a time? You message back and forth for a few days and then you don't hear from her for a week. Or two. What then?

In this connected world, it's really not true that someone who wants to reach you can't do so in the space of two weeks.

If that happens, it's a choice she's making. Other things in her life are more interesting or more important than reaching out to you.

Cut her loose and move on.

I know, she seems great. But chances are the girl has Plan B'ed you or just isn't that interested and doesn't know how to tell you.

What do I mean by Plan B'ed you? That's when a girl thinks you're somewhat interesting, but not as interesting as this other guy she's talking to. So she tries to string you along while she decides whether things with the other guy are going to work out. If they do, she disappears and you're left wondering what happened. If they don't, she turns her attention back to you until someone else new and shiny distracts her again.

You don't want to be with a girl who sees you as her second choice or her fallback plan. Move on and find a girl who thinks you're absolutely amazing.

And don't do this to women. If you're not that interested, cut her loose.

# WHEN TO MEET IN PERSON

So, when should you go on a date with a girl you've met online?

Sooner is probably better than later.

I tend to drag things out a bit because I don't want to meet up with a guy who turns out to be a psycho. Another friend of mine was out on first dates within a few days of joining a site.

If you communicate for too long without meeting up in person, the conversation tends to die off after a while. She has other options and you do, too, so if you aren't immediately interested she'll look elsewhere.

I also had at least one situation where the guy got a little too cozy about our e-mails and was suggesting a first date curled up on the couch in his basement watching movies. And another where he started telling me about his back aches and pain medicines. You don't want to go there, so meet up with her before you get too comfy, cozy.

Also, if you let the messaging back and forth go on for too long you may get so tied up with what you think this girl is that you fail to see who she really is. You have this beautiful picture in front of you and you imagine all sort of things that just aren't true. Only way to pop that bubble is to confront it with reality, which is best done sooner rather than later.

Remember, people do lie. For all you know, everything you

see in that profile is bullshit. And even if it isn't, there's this thing called in-person chemistry that matters more than most of us are willing to admit. A girl can seem great online and then you meet her in real life and it falls flat.

So exchange a few messages to make sure she's not insane and then agree to meet up.

It's okay. That's the point, right?

# CHOOSE A SAFE FIRST DATE

I advise women to be careful on their first date. You're a stranger to her and, unfortunate as this may be, women are more likely to be the victims of violence from a situation like this than men. So your role is to make her feel safe by suggesting a first date that doesn't come off as creepy. Like what?

## 1. MEET SOMEWHERE PUBLIC

Don't have her come to your house. Don't go to hers. Don't suggest meeting at the end of some remote trailhead for a hike.

## 2. CHOOSE A DATE THAT ALLOWS EITHER ONE OF YOU TO LEAVE WITH EASE

Don't go on a boat cruise. Don't fly her to another city in your private jet. (Haha.)

## 3. WATCH YOUR ALCOHOL OR DRUG USE

We each have our personal limits on this, but this is a stranger, and it might behoove you to stay aware of your surroundings and what's happening.

Those are the biggies. Basically, don't come off creepy and don't suggest something that isolates or threatens her. And don't make a concerted effort to dull her senses. If she wants to drink, fine, but don't be the guy pushing drinks on her or refilling her glass.

If you make it through three hours and it's going well, then let the date go where it may. But start off in a safe space and let her be the one to suggest taking it somewhere more private.

# SEX

You met someone online, you've hit it off, and now...You want to have sex.

First, think about your sexual safety. I'm not your mom, but I'm going to act like it for a minute. If you're going into online dating and you don't have strong moral or religious reasons for waiting to have sex, chances are that will be on the table at some point.

Do you have condoms? If not, buy a pack. You don't have to carry them with you for use on a moment's notice, but know that you have them and know where they are and if things are headed in that direction, steer the activity to where you can get them.

Now, maybe you don't like condoms. (Shock.)

If you're not using condoms, how are you protecting yourself from sexually-transmitted diseases? (Or is it sexually-transmitted infections these days? I'm showing my age, aren't I?)

Whatever you call them, STDs or STIs, how are you ensuring that you don't walk away from this experience with herpes or crabs or syphilis or whatever else is out there?

Condoms are very helpful in that respect. If you don't go the condom route, then maybe you go the testing route and you both get tested before you have sex.

Of course, that route presupposes that neither one of you are currently sexually active with other partners. Do you know that about her? Have you asked? Can you trust that she's told you the truth?

Do not assume that you know the answer to that question. And know that you're taking a risk if you believe her and don't have enough experience to judge the truth of her answer.

Make a mistake on this and you may have a lifetime to remember her.

The second thing you need to think about is pregnancy. Is she on birth control? If not, are you comfortable enough to just use condoms or should you wait until she's on something?

Usually that takes time.

With birth control pills she'll need to wait until the end of her cycle and start taking them and then they aren't really effective for about a month after that. Something like an IUD needs to be inserted by the doctor, which means waiting for the appointment, and then waiting a few more days until she can have sex.

Not fun, but best to think about it now than find yourself fathering a kid with a woman you hardly know.

And, no, you are never too old to have to think about these things. I don't know where I saw it, but the 60+ age range is at the top for acquiring STDs. It's great to have fun. Just be safe about it.

# WHEN TO HAVE SEX

So when should you have sex with someone you meet online?

Simple answer: Whenever you're comfortable doing so.

Now, having said that, and acknowledging that each relationship is different, in general, if you are looking for a long-term relationship, you should probably wait a few dates to have sex. Maybe even more than a few dates.

Sleep with a woman too soon and you risk flipping that switch in your brain that turns her from future mother of your children into good for a few nights. You could ruin something great if you're the type of guy to view a woman that way.

Not to mention, sex clouds your brain. When the sex is great it's easy to overlook all the ways you guys aren't compatible. All the little deal-breakers that are going to prevent this relationship from continuing already exist, but if you're in that heady glow from good sex, you'll gloss right over them.

So, as 50's housewife as it sounds, I say hold off a bit.

I would say you should wait at least three dates. In my personal experience, that's about when men stop trying to figure out how to sleep with me and start listening to what I'm actually telling them. Up until that point they'll nod and smile about anything I say, no matter how much it contradicts what they think.

Having said that, I also don't believe in artificially stopping something that's progressing well. Don't destroy a potential relationship by setting some arbitrary limits on yourself.

Do what you're comfortable with when you're comfortable with it.

# THE FIRST DATE

Here I went and talked about sex and we haven't even talked about the first date yet. I know this is a book about online dating, but that first date matters, too.

In my experience, most men default to the coffee date or drink date. It's annoying. I know some people think it's good because it lets you feel the person out without a lot of time or money committed. I get annoyed because the drink date is not really a drink date. It's a "drinks so I can see if you're worth dinner" date.

I say, be more creative. Suggest activity dates. Like a walk around a lake (in a nice public place) or bowling or pool or video games at the arcade or something that can be one or two hours but that lets you guys interact without the pressure of staring at each other trying to converse the whole time.

I'd also suggest that you pay. I know, old-school. But in my experience most men do pay. I always offer and I'm always prepared to back that offer up if needed, but I like men who pay for the first date. I think most women do.

If you're dealing with a woman who really does want to pay, then let her pay. This is how the two scenarios work:

The check comes. You immediately or very soon after (because the place you're at will keep checking back to see if you've paid yet) reach for the check and start to pay it.

The woman should reach for her wallet and offer to pay her share.

You say, "No, I've got it."

She says, "Are you sure?"

You say, "Yes."

She says, "Thank you."

Done.

If she wants to pay, she'll say, "No, I insist" instead of "Are you sure?" If she says that, let her pay. Some women feel the need to do so. I think most appreciate if a man pays. All my friends certainly do.

I know, dating is expensive, especially if you're expected to pay. That's where creative activity dates can come in handy. You don't have to spend money to walk around a lake. And many cities have free events if it's really that hard for you.

To me paying is part of wooing a woman. I'm treated as the equal of men every day at work. When I'm dating, I want to be treated special and I want to show the man I'm with that he can do things for me, that I'm not a hundred percent independent and capable. (Although I can be.)

But that's also the type of relationship I want. Not everyone does.

So I guess you should start how you want to finish. You don't believe in doing for your woman, then don't pay. It'll certainly narrow things down quickly to just your type of woman.

# CONCLUSION

That's about it. I've told you everything I can think of to help you get started. Let's see if we can't rehash it:

1. Be honest with yourself about what you want.

2. Be honest with others about what you want.

3. Be patient and persistent.

4. Be open to meeting women that aren't as attractive as you want.

5. Pick the right site or app for what you're looking for.

6. Remember people lie.

7. Align your user name/photos/profile.

8. Be yourself.

9. Avoid women who are damaged.

10. Be safe (sexually and otherwise).

11. Don't quit.

And, last, but not least, have fun with it.
   Good luck.

# Don't Be A Douchebag

# Douchebag

## Online Dating Advice I Wish Men Would Take

CASSIE LEIGH

# CONTENTS

# INTRODUCTION

Here's the deal. Online dating sucks. Half the time, the wrong people are talking to each other and it ends up turning into a real slog. You like someone, they shut you down, and you don't know why.

It can be frustrating. And hard. And time consuming.

This book is meant to help you avoid some of the common pitfalls of online dating from a woman who has been there, done that.

There are a few chapters in here for the legitimate douchebags (which I define as men who want some woman any woman to sleep with or who are so emotionally damaged that they can't handle a real relationship), because if those guys could target their efforts, it'd make the whole experience better for all of us.

So, if you do just want some fun sexy times, stick to the first few chapters. If not, if you really want to find a woman for a lasting relationship, then this book can help. It'll get you past the worst offenses men commit.

I'm not a kind and gentle soul, but if you listen to what I have to say, you'll do better, I promise.

So, with that said, let's get started.

# SETTING THE STAGE

First, you need to understand what online dating is like for a reasonably attractive woman.

Let's assume that we're not on one of those sites that structure your communications. It's just a free-for-all, contact-anyone-you-want-say-anything-you-want, situation.

Maybe this woman created a profile last night because she thought it would be fun to see what her personality type is.

(I made that mistake once.)

Or maybe she finally decided that joining that gym wasn't going to result in any romantic possibilities and it was time to give online dating a chance.

Whatever the reason, she creates a profile, puts up a picture that her guy friends like, fills in answers to all the questions (even the stupid ones), and goes to sleep.

She isn't looking for a casual hookup. She wants a relationship. And she says so right there in her profile.

This is what she finds when she wakes up:

*You have 22 new messages from The Best Dating Site in the World!*

At first, she's excited.

Twenty-two messages! Wow. That's great.

She thought she'd get one or two messages, but twenty-two? There's bound to be someone interesting in there.

She opens the first one.

It's from a guy who explains that he's married and staying in the relationship for the kids, but that he really needs to get some lovin' so he's joined this site looking for someone to sleep with on the side. He saw her profile and found her very attractive.

He, of course, doesn't have a picture on his profile because he doesn't want anyone to know that he's a cheating bastard (my words, not his), but he'd be happy to send a picture along if she's interested.

Right, because obviously she is so desperate to find someone that she'll agree to screwing around with a married man. No.

Delete.

She opens the second one.

It says, "Hey hottie! Whatcha up to tonight?"

She looks and can see that it was sent about a minute after she uploaded her profile picture.

Great to see he couldn't take the time to look at anything other than her photo. Delete.

E-mail three is an obvious cut and paste about the guy. "My name is John and I am thirty-two. I like long walks and am looking for a woman to walk with me through life."

Couldn't even take the time to find just one little thing they might have in common and add it to his obvious form message?

Delete.

E-mails four through ten are a variation on e-mails two and three.

Delete. Delete. Delete...

E-mail eleven is another with no profile picture from a guy asking her if she's into younger men.

Delete.

E-mail twelve is from a man about twenty years older than her who says he's looking for someone to have great sex with. His profile picture shows him with a deep tan and a very large boat.

He seems to think this makes him unique or special because he can be upfront about what he's looking for.

Ha! Right. 'Cause no other guy on the site is looking for sex. They just want someone to hold hands with.

Delete.

E-mail thirteen is a long e-mail from a man explaining how much he likes to please women and is looking for someone who will take a firm hand with him.

Ew. Delete.

While reading the first batch of e-mails she's seeing out of the corner of her eye that more men are checking out her profile.

By the time she finishes e-mail fourteen, she has five new messages—all of the "Hey sexy-what's up?" variety.

Delete. Delete. Delete…

If she's new to this, she may actually try to respond to some of these guys.

Nothing wrong with a guy who thinks you're attractive and shoots off a quick e-mail, right?

Wrong.

She'll learn.

Because if she does write back and try to say anything about what's in her profile—"Sorry, I didn't respond last night. I had to go to salsa classes"—she'll either get no response because the guy was just looking for someone to hook up with right then or she'll get a response that shows that the guy still hasn't read her profile—"So, you do salsa, huh? Cool. Whatcha up to?"

So, here we are. She's read and deleted twenty messages so far.

And now she opens yours.

She's not at her best right now.

She's wondering why she bothers.

She's starting to think she should've just hooked up with that obnoxious frat guy in college who cornered her at that party.

She's thinking that at least if you date a co-worker you know that he can act normal five days out of seven.

She's on the edge.

If you're going to get through to her, you need to be a refreshing ray of sunlight in the dark hell in which she's found herself.

The rest of this book will discuss how you do that. But first we need to cover the douchebags.

(If you want to skip past the chapters for the douchebags, which might be entertaining, but not of much use in terms of advice, go to Chapter 4: So You Really Want to Find Someone.)

# SO YOU ARE A DOUCHEBAG

Nothing wrong with that. It takes all types.

What do I mean by this? Well, you're the type of guy who sees women as interchangeable and only good for one thing—satisfying your ego or fucking.

You don't want to get to know someone.

You don't want to form a connection.

You just want to get your rocks off.

That's cool. Why you're reading this book is beyond me, but, whatever. Your money, not mine.

Maybe you'd like to be that kind of guy—the guy who can go online and find someone for the weekend— but you just don't know how to make that happen.

Okay. Let's walk through how this works.

First, the rest of this book is not for you. Because getting laid (if that's all you want) is just a numbers game.

If a woman wants to have sex, what you say isn't all that relevant.

(Try not to be a dumbass and say really offensive things, but, other than that, it doesn't matter much.)

Do you need brilliant pick-up lines?

("Is your father a thief? Did he steal the stars and put them in your eyes?" Okay, so maybe that's not a brilliant one. But use it on a woman when she wants to like you and she'll laugh and you'll think it is.)

No. Brilliance is not required.

This is about sex, not compatibility.

All you need to do is keep going until you find someone who says, "yes."

Don't waste time building up to the question and go back and forth with some woman for a week or two.

(You probably shouldn't ask it in the first message, though. I suspect that might get you banned from some sites.)

So, a few back and forths, a "Hey, wanta hang out?" sent at two in the morning, and move on to the next until one says, "Sure, why not?"

This is where all the "Hey, hottie" messages come from. Guys who don't give a shit who they're talking to.

(If you do give a shit, now you know why that approach doesn't work for guys like you—because it makes you look like one of the douchebags.)

So, like I said, it's a numbers game. Send enough messages to enough women, you will find one to sleep with.

And, great for both of you. I have no problem with people looking for sex who find other people looking for sex.

I just wish they'd leave me out of it.

And how do you leave someone like me out of it?

By taking *ten seconds* to look at the profile of the woman you're about to message.

(Trust me, it'll be worth it. You'll up your hit percentage.)

What do you look for?

Boobs. Fish lips. Obvious selfies. A girl who posts pictures of herself at the bar with ten of her besties or surrounded by tons of guys.

(If the guys are shirtless or sleeveless, add a few extra bonus points.)

Scan the woman's profile.

Lots of text? Not your girl.

Your girl doesn't need to say much more than that she's "fun", "likes to party", and "wants to have a good time."

If she can't spell, even better.

A note here: There will be other women who want to just find someone for sex. Professional types that aren't going to post boob and selfie photos.

Chances are those women will be a little more discreet and focused in what they do, because the last thing they need is a boss or co-worker to see their profile and think the wrong thing.

You may just need to let those women come to you.

What we're talking about here are the low-hanging fruit.

So, to sum up: You want a chick showing off her boobs, making a kissy face at the camera, talking about how much fun she is.

And if there's a picture of her doing shots? Bonus.

Now, some of you are a very special kind of douchebag— you're married or otherwise in a committed relationship and looking for something on the side.

Guess what? You get your very own chapter. Lucky you!

# SO YOU'RE MARRIED

Fuck you. Leave me alone.

Okay, now that we've gotten past that. Let's chat.

You're married or you've been living with a woman for years. And it isn't enough for you.

The love is gone. She no longer wants to have sex. You're tired of all of your lovey dovey time involving *Playboy* magazine and your own hand.

Got it.

I'm sorry that life sucks so bad for you.

But why are you contacting this woman?

Did you see the part in her profile where she said she wanted a relationship? And, no, screwing you twice a week when it's convenient and you can get away with it is not what she meant.

There are women who like screwing married men.

There are women who like screwing any and all men. (See previous chapter.)

Find one of them.

Oh, but you're *special*. You need to have a *connection* with a woman and those brainless party girls just aren't enough for you.

You want a woman with substance—an intelligent, funny, witty woman who can have a scintillating conversation *and* orgasmic sex.

Here's your problem: She's intelligent, funny, witty, and looking for a real relationship.

Do you really think she wants to get involved with you? No. No, she does not.

Now, some women who meet all of the above criteria do make stupid choices. But they generally don't do so online with some stranger they've never met.

They get a little too close to that co-worker when they're working on that high-stress, all-hours project. Or they find themselves drawn to that funny and charming guy on their kickball team.

They do not, as a general rule, respond to married douchebags trolling for women on dating sites.

If you can't just settle for one of the women who would happily screw you and instead have to go for one of the women who really, really does not want to get involved with a guy like you, then you need to develop that in the real world, not online.

You could lie. You could pretend to be single until she's so far under your spell that she goes against her better instincts, but you're playing with fire.

Because if you've misjudged, this is the type of woman who will burn you hard when she finds out.

Call your wife, hard. Call your boss, hard.

Grab you by the balls and twist, hard.

Don't do it. It's not worth it.

What you need to do is find a woman who is expressly looking for a douche like you.

How do you do this?

Well, I'm not going to name any sites here, but there are sites out there that will let you find a woman like this.

First, there are the obvious ones that are specifically geared toward committed types like you.

(If you don't know which ones I'm talking about, I wonder if you ever watch the news or have any friends.)

Second, there's also at least one mainstream site that has questions designed to let you find those types of women. (And it's free, too!)

This is what you do. You go to that free site and you find the questions that say, "I want to screw around with a guy who's already in a relationship" and you tell the site that you want women who answered that question "YES, PLEASE! SOUNDS AWESOME."

You make that of utmost importance for your match results. And, for every possible match, you see how the woman you're about to approach answered that question *before* you reach out to her.

You don't waste your time messaging women who answered, "HELL NO. THAT GUY WOULD BE A SCUM BUCKET THAT I WOULDN'T TOUCH WITH A TEN-FOOT POLE."

Got it? Pretty simple.

There are women out there who want this kind of thing. Please find them and leave the rest of us alone.

(Oh, and if you're not just looking for sex with anyone living and of the opposite sex who meets your general physical requirements, have you stopped to think that maybe, just maybe it isn't sex that's lacking in your relationship? Maybe instead of looking for some strange online you should put some effort into your relationship and fix your shit instead? Or, dare I say it, move on?)

(Maybe your wife no longer wants to sleep with you because you've become a passive-aggressive asshole or a distant, entitled jerk. Just a thought.)

(And, no, I don't feel bad for insulting you. You made a commitment to someone and you are now lying and cheating and deceiving them. I have no sympathy for you. I wouldn't even play the world's smallest violin for you. Fix your shit.)

If you have permission from your significant other, that's a different story.

I still don't want to get involved with you, but I don't think you're pond scum. You're just fishing off the wrong pier.

Join a polyamory group or look for women open to that kind of thing. Just leave those of us who want committed monogamous one-to-one relationships out of it, okay?

# SO YOU REALLY WANT TO FIND SOMEONE

Good. We've got some work to do, but, hopefully, by the end of this book you'll have a lot better idea of what triggers a woman to delete your messages.

Keep in mind, though, that this is just one woman's perspective. Other women may feel differently about some of these issues.

What's key (and it'll come up repeatedly throughout the rest of this book) is that you listen to the woman you are approaching. Look at her pictures, her user name, what she says in her profile, and her e-mails to you.

*Listen.*

And remember that this is from the viewpoint of the woman who barely convinced herself to try this whole online dating thing.

She's living her life happily enough but wouldn't mind finding someone to share it with.

She's not going to take a lot of shit. She's not going to give a guy a chance just because "you never know."

This is a woman who can get by just fine. She pays her own bills and has an education and career.

She doesn't need to be saved.

She isn't desperately lonely.

She gets enough male attention in the real world, so she isn't on there to get her ego stroked.

She'd just kinda, sorta like to find someone she can click with.

So, how do you present yourself as the guy she's looking for?

Well, let's start at the beginning.

# STEP ONE –
# IS SHE A GOOD FIT FOR YOU?

First things first, you need to decide whether this woman is a good fit for *you*.

Of course she is. Look at that smile. Isn't she pretty?

She looks like a nice person, doesn't she?

The type who'd sit across the table from you and listen sympathetically while you talk about what a tough day you had at work.

STOP.

Stop right there.

Let's figure out what it is that you actually want.

Do you like women who cuss? No? *Have you looked at her profile?*

I can't count all that high, but it seems to me that there's a lot of damn and shit being used there. Do you imagine that this woman's not going to cuss in person when she does in her profile?

Do you like women who are active? Yes? Okay, *have you looked at her profile?*

What's that say under hobbies? Reading, board games, and Tetris. Is that an active woman?

Or, on the flip side, when was the last time you went for a hike? Three years ago?

Nothing wrong with that, but what are you doing imagining that the woman who lists her hobbies as rock climbing and marathon running is going to be a good match?

Maybe you do share a ton of interests. Great.

Is she nice?

Look, my profile reads a lot like this book. I'm snarky and obnoxious and fairly hostile. And yet I get men who are clearly accommodating and sweet writing me all the time. Why??

I'm not a mean person. I don't like to hurt people. But dealing with a sweet guy like that makes me feel as bad as kicking a puppy.

I've never kicked a puppy, by the way. But I have certainly had to shut down a perfectly nice, innocuous guy because he was clearly not going to be able to deal with me as I am.

If you're a nice guy and you aren't looking for a nice girl, you need to reconsider what you're doing.

It's not that nice guys finish last. It's that nice guys are just like any other guy and they focus far too much on physical appearance and far too little on compatibility, so end up chasing the wrong women.

Stop doing that.

Find someone who shares your interests.

Someone with a similar outlook and perspective.

A woman with the same values as you.

You're not going to listen to me, but I'm telling you:

***Ignore the picture.***

Not forever!

Just long enough to see if she's compatible.

This is the approach you should take:

Compatible? Yes. Attractive? Yes. Okay, reach out.

What most men do:

Attractive? Yes. Reach out.

Don't do that to yourself. The information is there, use it.

# STEP TWO –
# BE WHO YOU ARE

In my last foray into online dating I saw at least two profiles where the guys were over forty but listed their ages as thirty-nine because they didn't want to get left out of searches.

Bullshit. Those guys were insecure. They turned forty and it freaked them out, so they thought the best approach was to lie about it.

You know what that tells me about them? That they're liars.

And guys who lie are douchebags.

There is no "turning forty" exception. A lie is a lie.

What else is that guy going to lie about?

So he was a little paranoid that turning forty meant women in their thirties wouldn't want him anymore.

(Wrong, by the way. And even more wrong when it comes to certain women in their twenties.)

It was a little lie, he admitted it in his profile. No big deal, right?

Wrong.

Here's the deal. We're talking about people looking for a relationship here. This should be built upon openness and trust.

If some guy thinks it's no big deal to lie about his age, what else will he lie about?

What happens when he loses his job?

Is he one of those guys that will pretend to still have a job, dress up in his suit every morning, and go sit at Starbucks all day rather than tell his partner that he's unemployed?

That's not what a woman wants. She hasn't even met this guy yet and he's already broken her trust.

BE WHO YOU ARE.

Own it. List your real hobbies. List your real profession.

Do not say you're a lawyer, when you're just an assistant to one. (True example, by the way.)

Do not say you draw comics when you drew one comic two years ago. (Another true example.)

A woman who is looking for a real relationship is going to pay attention to what you say. And she'll believe it, too.

If you lie to this woman, she'll walk away.

This myth that you can make a woman fall in love with you and then tell her the truth is a bunch of crap. That is one shaky foundation to build a relationship on.

I'm not saying all women will judge you for a lie or walk away the first time they catch you out.

*They should.*

Unfortunately, there are lots of forgiving types out there who will probably let it slide.

But is that what you want? To live a lie? To be insecure all the time with the one person who should have your back?

Fake it for the rest of the world, but don't fake it for your partner.

It will collapse at some point and it won't be pretty.

So, own who you are.

Even if it is someone over forty who weighs fifty pounds more than they did ten years ago.

# STEP THREE –
## CHOOSE THE RIGHT PICTURE

So, you've found someone you like and you want to message her. Good.

First, let's talk about your pictures.

It's tempting, I know it is, to post that picture of you from ten years ago where you looked really frickin' hot.

But that's not who you are now. That's who you were on one day ten years ago.

Let it go.

Be yourself.

Post a current photo. You're not twenty-two anymore. You no longer run around with a killer tan and board shorts all summer.

As a matter of fact, the last time you wore board shorts was in that photo. So, stop it.

Show who you are NOW.

So what if that's a mid-thirties, office-bound, computer nerd? Own it.

You aren't going to be on the cover of GQ anytime soon. And? So? Does that matter? No.

Are you charming? Can you make a woman laugh? *That* matters.

Your looks are just part of the equation. And they are what they are.

Unless you were planning on getting plastic surgery or inventing a time machine before that first date?

No? Well then...

Post an accurate photo!

Fact of the matter is that confidence will do far more for you than all the plastic surgery in the world.

Now, step back and look at that photo.

Does it reflect who you are?

Does it show what your interests are? What you value?

Too often men feel this need to post photos of themselves looking fun or athletic. So they post that one photo of that one party they went to a year ago even though they're much more the quiet dinner at home type.

(I can't count the number of tuxedo photos I've seen that were from some wedding the guy attended.)

Or they put up a photo of that one tandem skydive they did five years ago that they only did because their best friend threatened to publish certain photos from college if they didn't agree to it.

If it's not representative of you, don't use it.

Don't get me wrong. If you do adventurous things with your life and want to post pictures that show that and some are one-offs, that's fine.

But if you've done two adventurous things in your entire life and those are the pictures you choose to post, you're just creating a false impression of yourself that you now have to live up to.

Another true story: I had some guy reach out to me who it turns out was a fairly successful and interesting entrepreneur.

His profile picture (and user name) made him look like a street punk. Baseball cap tilted to the side, baggy clothes. I think he was even throwing a "hang tough" sign.

The guy in that photo was of no interest to me.

And this guy wasn't even like that anymore. But that's what he was showing to prospective partners, which probably wasn't helping him much.

Oh, and, no matter how bad you look, post a photo.

If you have something seriously wrong with you, I know that's tough to do. It probably means lots of rejection, because many women will judge you based on that photo.

But if it's something that will drive women away from even responding to you, you're probably better off meeting someone in real life and not even trying online dating.

(I know. Scary thought. But letting someone get to know you in real life really can overcome an amazing number of flaws and quirks that people will reject you for online.)

Once again: this idea that you can get a woman to fall in love with you and then reveal the "real you" is BULLSHIT. Especially if you think it can happen online without any in-person contact.

I'm sure it sucks to not be traditionally attractive. But all you have to do is go to the grocery store some weekend and look around at all the couples. There really is someone for everyone.

Can you get a Victoria's Secret model? Well, are you a billionaire with a great sense of humor? Or Jason Statham? No? Then, probably not.

But you can find *someone*. And it'll be a hell of a lot easier to find that person if you're up front with what you look like and who you are *now*.

# STEP FOUR –
# CHECK YOUR PROFILE

Before you actually message this woman, let's take a quick peek at your profile.

"My friends say I'm a bit of a loner. Lol."

What is that shit?

Did you really *laugh out loud* when you wrote that? No. You did not.

(If you did, may I suggest some counseling?)

Look. Men use "lol" *all the frickin' time*. And *always* in ways like I cited above.

(Yes, that's hyperbole. Deal with it.)

Using "lol" like that makes a man look like a nervous serial killer.

Don't do it.

Go through your profile and eliminate every single "lol."

Every. Single. One.

You don't want to? Fine. Just know that you will not get started with a woman like me if you leave them in.

I see "lol" in a profile and I think insecure, young, clueless, nervous, or lacking in social skills.

Is that the impression you want to make?

No.
You're better than that.
(At least I hope you are.)
So, show it.

# STEP FIVE –
## SHOW SOME CONFIDENCE

Let's chat about this whole you being you thing again.

Here's the deal: You're only going to find someone you're compatible with if you're honest about who you are.

Me? I'm looking at everything you put up on that site to get a feel for you. I look at your pictures, what you write about yourself, your personality profile if there is one, and any questions you answer.

One of the sites I've been on asks some crazy shit. You know the one, right?

The one that wants to know if you cross-dress or like golden showers or would be willing to make loud animal noises during sex if your partner asked?

If that's not your deal, it's *okay to say no.*

It's okay to say that not in a million years would you let someone pee on you.

That doesn't make you boring. That just makes you someone who doesn't like to be peed on.

It's fine. Really, it is.

(Women might even like you for that. I certainly would.)

Own who you are.

Look, the "cool kids" don't know what the fuck they're doing half the time. Stop trying to be one of them and find a way to live your life in a way that works for you.

True story time.

Some guy messaged me and he looked all conservative and nervous in his profile. Recently divorced, accountant-type.

Nothing in his answers indicated any sort of kinky inclinations.

But those crazy questions above? He said he'd be open to trying all of them.

Now, nothing wrong with that if it's true. Maybe he was tired of being a conservative person and was willing to try whatever. Cool.

(I wasn't going to go there with him, but you know, whatever.)

Except, that wasn't the case.

I asked him about it, because that's the type of woman I am.

And he said it wasn't really something he had an interest in doing, but he didn't want to rule anything out.

To me, he was just trying to be a pleaser.

In doing so, he lost my respect and interest.

Be who you are.

Nine times out of ten a woman will like you more for being your own person than she will for being some limp noodle that bends at the slightest indication of difference.

A secret (and let's remember the type of woman we're dealing with here—confident, has her shit together, looking for an equal): You don't always have to bend over backwards to make a woman happy.

A woman wants a man who has his own opinions and interests and who occasionally disagrees with her.

That makes him an *equal* not some fawning sycophant with no identifiable personality of his own.

Harsh?

Yes.

But true.

An unwillingness to say who he is and stick to it is one of the worst traits a man can have.

(Being a dick is probably number one. But being spineless is a close second. There's a balance there. It *is* possible to accommodate another person without losing who you are.)

(And it's this willingness to please at all costs that make people think nice guys finish last. They don't lose because they're nice. They lose because they're not their own person.)

# A LITTLE DIGRESSION ON COMMUNICATION

Time to remind you that we're talking about women like me and appealing to women like me. If you're eighteen and trying to pick up women online (why you're not doing so in the real world, I don't know), then maybe this advice isn't for you.

Because there's a generational gap here and young women may not write the same way I do.

So, here's the lesson to learn: People communicate in different ways. You want to signal to this woman that you are like her, which means you want to communicate in the same way she does.

I, and women like me, write sentences with capital letters and punctuation. I spell things correctly. I use proper grammar. I do not use "lol."

I'm pretty sure my profile doesn't have any smiley faces in it either (although my e-mails and chats do).

Other women will be different. Other women will use lol and no capitalization and exclamation points everywhere.

So what do you do when you find a woman you like?

You look at how she communicates and mirror her communication style.

(Just like with body language when you're in person, mirroring someone's form of writing will make them feel more compatible with you.)

Ideally, you would create a profile that is true to who you are and then seek out women who match that, so you wouldn't even have to think about this.

But if you can't quite bring yourself to do that (because look at that smile!), then at least try to craft your messages to her in a way that will capture her interest.

(Or, at a minimum, not repel her.)

(And if using "lol" eight million times is your style, then own it. Just know that you're limiting your pool of potential matches.)

# STEP SIX –
## TIME TO MAKE CONTACT

Wait. Before you send that e-mail, let's have a chat.

You need to understand something before you reach out to this woman. (Who is hopefully *compatible* with you as well as attractive?)

Here's the deal:

*You are a random stranger on the Internet.*

That's right. You are a potentially crazy, psycho stalker.

I know, I know. *You're* not.

But as far as she knows you could be.

So, dial it back a notch.

Don't assume that just because you saw her picture and immediately started thinking about creative uses for whipped cream or romantic evenings cuddled together by the fire that she thought the same thing when she saw yours.

Yes, this is online dating and you know far more about her than you would if you met her at a bar, but *you don't know her.*

So don't presume to.

When you meet a woman in the real world, do you talk to her about the vacations you'll take together?

Or about meeting your family?

Or long walks on the beach with no one else around?

No? Good.

(You shouldn't. That's creepy shit if you do.)

So, why would you act any different online?

Sure, you've exchanged a ton of e-mails with this woman, but you don't know her and she doesn't know you.

Do not presume sex.

Do not presume intimacy.

Don't talk about how good you are at massages.

(Time enough for her to find out about your magic hands later.)

Don't suggest a first date that is more appropriate for a long-term couple.

(This means no dinner at your place or her place, nothing isolated, and nothing involving your family. I know you just got out of a seven-year relationship and you miss all of that, but this woman is not your ex, so back off and give her a little space.)

Yeah, we're getting a little ahead of ourselves here.

I mean, you haven't even messaged this woman yet and here I am telling you how to handle your first date. But you have to nail this stuff right from the start.

First message to last, you have to know what you're doing.

And I will tell you that many a man falls flat on his face because he's too eager to get to the in-person payoff.

Another true story:

I was exchanging messages with a guy who at first looked pretty promising.

Until he started talking about how he was looking forward to snuggling up with me under a blanket in his basement and watching movies.

Ew. No. That is not appealing coming from a guy I've never even met.

So, stay calm.

Breathe.

Back off a bit.

This woman is a stranger.

You need to intrigue her enough that she wants to meet you, not drive her away with an over the top need to create an insta-relationship or get laid.

Now, someone who didn't read the first few chapters of this book and is sitting here saying, "But, that's so wrong. Because I had this chick I was messaging and we totally had great chat sex before we ever met. So, you're wrong. Women want sex with complete strangers, too."

"And there are all sorts of articles out there about how women will totally have sex on the first date. It's like the norm now."

May I direct your attention to the *So You Are A Douchebag* chapter?

Those women—the ones who have sex with a guy within hours of meeting him in person for the first time—are not who we're talking about here.

This book is about getting the woman who shuts you down when you ask her for a fun photo before you've ever met.

This is the woman who tried to politely remind you that you're still basically strangers when you suggested Sunday dinner with your extended family for that first date.

You do not know this woman. So stop acting like you do.

Oh, and this book isn't going to go into how to handle dating this woman, but just a quick pointer: When you do meet this woman, remember that it's the first time she's met you.

If you don't think she's the type to go home from a bar with a complete stranger, it's probably safe to assume she isn't going home with you on that first date.

Try to actually listen to what she's saying instead of steering the conversation towards sex every chance you get.

(Trust me, it may seem counterintuitive, but doing so will probably up your chance of eventually sleeping with this woman.)

Okay. So, now you know to dial back the intimacy/sex conversations for a bit.

What else do you need to know before you message her?

# KEEP YOUR COOL

Do not let this woman see you sweat.

Have you ever been confronted by a bear in the wilderness?

No? Me neither.

But I do remember what I've read about how to handle a situation like that.

You stand tall, you own your space, you don't make aggressive eye contact, and you bluff the shit out of the situation.

Same rules apply here.

Because if you show a woman like this that you doubt yourself, she will eat you alive.

(Remember, we're not talking about the sweet, accommodating, nice to everyone woman here. We're talking about that other kind of woman. The one who isn't afraid to say "No, thank you" and walk away.)

Let's say this woman is more attractive than you.

And? So what?

Maybe she's better educated.

Again. Who cares?

She might even be more successful than you.

Does it matter? No.

So, she has it all and you're a couch-surfing bum that can't keep a job.

What do you do?

Fake it, buddy. Pretend that it doesn't mean anything.

So what if she's a Fortune 500 CEO and you work at McDonald's?

You're funny and great at Trivial Pursuit.

Who's to say which is more important?

What you do not do under any circumstances is say, "Wow, you're so much smarter than me."

Or, "Gee, I can't believe a woman as attractive as you would date me."

A real one I received once: "Man, I sure hope you at least enjoyed that date a little bit. I sure did."

I hadn't minded the date. I might've even gone out on another one with the guy.

Until I got that e-mail.

And then I realized I was dealing with a guy who'd been insecure about being there.

(And he didn't even know the half of it.)

Quick point: Men will brag on their dating profiles about how successful, educated, and everything else they are. Women won't.

Which means however impressive she seems at first glance, you should probably double that for everything except her appearance.

So, back to the point: Never let her see you doubt your right to be with her.

(This is pretty much true of everything in life, by the way. Job interviews. Business meetings. Choosing teams at recess…)

If you don't feel it, fake it.

Yes, I know.

You want someone you can be honest with. Someone who can see the true you and still love you.

That will happen. But not yet.

First, you have to show her that you're her equal.

And you are. Believe it.

I'm not saying lie about who are. I'm saying be confident in who you are.

Do not apologize for being the wonderful, fantastic, unique individual you are.

Look.

We all have doubts and fears.

We all think we're inadequate in some way or another.

But should you show that in your online profile? No.

In your messages? No.

First date? Nope.

Wait until you're in a relationship.

Think of it this way: You're trying to date a tiger. Do you really want it to think that you're a bunny rabbit?

No. No, you do not.

# THE MESSAGE: PART ONE –
## SHE'S NOT STUPID

I know it's tempting to craft that perfect message and then just copy and paste it every time you see a promising profile.

DON'T.

This woman's not stupid. And she's not a factory-produced Barbie doll.

Look at her profile and then write something relevant and *personal*.

I know. It takes time.

But you're not a douchebag, right? You're not playing the numbers game?

You're actually looking for a woman who is compatible with you as well as being attractive?

Well, how many women really fit your criteria?

Not that many. (Or at least there shouldn't be.)

Which means you can take a few minutes and write a personalized message.

Why doesn't a copy and paste work?

Because, right from the start, you're telling this woman that you don't see her as an individual.

A man who uses copy and paste is a selfish fuck who's too

busy to spend enough time to personalize his message. He just wants someone, anyone.

I know. That's not actually why men do it.

But that's what she thinks. (Or at least what I think.)

Some men are nervous and decide this is the only way to make a good first impression.

They've vetted it with their friends, thought about it for a week or two, and rewritten it ten times until it's perfect.

But, it's not.

When you use copy and paste, you're not being you. You're not interacting with the woman you see in front of you.

It's like meeting a woman at a bar and pulling out index cards with canned phrases on them.

You wouldn't do that would you?

(Please tell me you wouldn't do that.)

Maybe your initial approach is stilted and awkward.

So?

That's fine. If that's you, then that's you.

I know, I know. You're thinking that it's not fine.

Because when you tried to message women without that copy and paste they rejected you.

But what you don't understand is that you're just prolonging the inevitable if you do somehow manage to get in with that first form message.

Because now she wrote you back. And you have to respond.

Shit. What do you do now?

Have a friend write the message for you?

Are they going to read *every* message before you send it?

How long can that last?

Will you ask them to review your twentieth anniversary card, too? (No.)

What if she wants to chat and you have to respond real-time?

You're screwed.

Because you weren't being you.

So, scrap the copy and paste. Read her profile and write something relevant to what she said.

It's not that hard.

And, remember, one of the reasons you want to do this is because you don't want to be confused with the douchebags.

Don't forget what it's like for her.

See, the thing is, your fellow man is making this shit ten times harder for you than it needs to be.

You know how sometimes you compliment a pretty woman on the street and she hardly reacts?

It's because some asswipe before you complimented her on her outfit and when she said, "Thank-you" and smiled at him he followed it up with a disgusting offer about what he'd be more than happy to do to her should she be willing.

She probably blew it off the first time it happened. Maybe even the second. But eventually she got sick of it.

So now she just ignores all men who compliment her in public, because there are more creepy sleazeballs than genuine nice guys out there.

Well, you're dealing with that same issue online.

The guy who messages women indiscriminately and follows any flicker of interest up with an inappropriate comment or request for fun photos is the reason you need to put a little time and effort into this thing.

You need to show her that you're not *that guy*.

# THE MESSSAGE: PART TWO –
# YOU'RE NOT STUPID EITHER
# (I HOPE)

Remember the type of woman we're talking about here. She writes with periods and capital letters. She uses proper grammar. She spells things correctly.

So you need to do so, too.

She may not be perfect in this respect.

But, in general, a woman like this is going to expect you to get the basics right.

You're thinking, what does it matter?

Who really cares about you're vs. your?

It's not like your entire married life is going to involve e-mailing one another.

Fair point.

(But then why choose a medium for meeting someone that highlights your weakness?)

This is why you do it: It shows you care.

(And, if you have a professional job, it shows that maybe you care about your career, too. Because how can you be an executive or a lawyer and not know basic grammar?)

(I hated grammar in school, but I wanted to succeed in my

career, so I learned that shit. If you have a job that involves writing, you should have, too.)

So, what are the basics?

## You're vs. your.

These contraction ones are pretty easy.

You're=you are. If you see you're and you can't replace it with you are, then you have the wrong word.

Think, "you're cool" vs. "I want to borrow your car."

## It's vs. its.

Same thing. It's=it is or it has. If you can't substitute it is or it has for it's, then you have the wrong word.

Think, "It's hard to do this shit" vs. "Don't let your dog lick its privates in front of your date."

(Yes, that's an icky example, but it'll probably stick with you, won't it?)

## Who's vs. whose.

Yet again. Who's=who is or who has. If you can't substitute it, you've got the wrong one.

Think, "Who's coming to dinner?" vs. "Whose car keys are these?"

## To vs. too vs. two.

Easy one first—two is a number.

(If you can't get that one right…man.)

Now, to vs. too. Too as in also. "Me, too."

To as in, "where are we going to."

(They're different parts of speech, but quite frankly explaining it using parts of speech is about as useful to me as someone telling me a food is a carb instead of a protein. Huh? Whatever. Okay…)

Look, I'm not a grammar expert. Find someone who is. Or read a grammar book.

Getting just these few words right will exponentially increase your odds of success with a woman like this.

A slip here or there isn't going to be an issue.

But repeated failures will.

Plus, getting this right is going to help you in the real world.

Imagine the impression you're making on your boss right now (assuming your boss knows this stuff).

Imagine what your clients think of you.

Learn it.

Or realize that it will limit your opportunities both with online dating and in the real world.

And no SAT words if you can't use them properly!

If they come to you naturally, then fine.

But there is nothing more obvious than the person who throws fancy schmancy words into the mix to try to appear more intelligent.

(Perfect example, go read an internet forum where a discussion has devolved into a petty "I'm right. You're wrong" back and forth. Guaranteed there will be at least one person in there trying to show that they should win the argument because they can use big words.)

I know it's a pain to learn this stuff. But if written communication isn't your thing, then don't use online dating.

Go to a bar. Join a sports team. Join MENSA. (Because, yes, sometimes smart people suck at writing.)

Do something in the real world that involves talking to someone in person.

Let a woman fall for your dreamy eyes and witty jokes instead of letting her judge you for your lack of capitalization and inability to use a period or start a new paragraph.

Play to your strengths.

But if you're going to stick with online dating, then master these basics.

Think of it as the equivalent of learning a hook shot in basketball. Or being able to hit a curve ball in baseball.

Sure, you can play the game without those skills, but you won't make it as far as you would with them.

# THE MESSAGE: PART THREE-
## YES, SHE'S PRETTY
## NO, YOU DON'T NEED TO TELL HER

Let's make a bold assumption here. You only want to date women that you're attracted to. Let's also assume that the women you reach out to know this.

(And let's remember that the type of woman we're talking about here is not the needy type that finds her worth through external validation. This advice does not apply to those types. Those types need compliments *all the time*.)

So, you find her attractive and she's pretty sure you find her attractive because you messaged her.

Back off the compliments.

I know. That's weird and counterintuitive, especially in our culture that values looks so highly.

But we're talking about a woman who has more going on than just her looks.

And, quite frankly, she's probably a little sick and tired at this point of men focusing on how pretty she is and missing everything else about her.

So don't be one of those guys.

Show her that you're different. Show her that you can see the whole package.

Let's go back to the bar analogy.

You're the online equivalent of the guy who chats her up on her way to the bathroom.

She's on a dating site, so she's open to being approached. But which approach do you think is more successful: "Hey, hottie, nice legs" or "Hey, I see that you went to Duke. So did I. What year?"

We've already established that she's not looking for a one-nighter, right? So....

She's going to prefer the guy that wants to make a real connection with her.

Be that guy.

You're playing the slow game. You can take your time.

It's not that women don't like to be complimented. Just limit it early on.

You can tell her she looks beautiful when you meet for your date, but right now you need to make a connection first. Show her that you can see past her appearance.

I can't emphasize this enough.

Let's say you're really struggling with this one.

You really want to compliment her. I mean, look at that smile. Can't you just compliment her smile?

Fine.

Here's what you do.

Tell her you really liked that picture of her doing whatever.

And then ask about it.

"I really loved that photo of you water skiing. Where was it taken?"

Or, "I go water skiing at the Reservoir at least every other weekend. Have you ever been?"

Now, some pictures make that hard. My profile picture is a close-up headshot, so there's really nothing to comment on other than my appearance.

In that case, you might, might, be able to get away with a "nice smile." But err on the side of caution.

(And please don't let that be the entire content of your message. Did you read her profile? She gave you so many things to comment on. Pick one.)

Remember who you're dealing with here.

This is a woman who's secure in herself. She appreciates that you find her attractive, but telling her that at the expense of making a genuine connection is not going to earn you any brownie points.

Oh, and for any of you who happen to have picked up certain dating advice books written by men who wear aviator glasses and fur coats in DC in June—this is not that "neg" thing.

We're not talking about insulting her.

This is about doing what most men don't do and looking past the picture to the woman behind the sexy hair and great smile.

Look. There *are* women out there who will soak up every single comment you throw their way and want more.

But not this woman.

You need to be able to tell the difference between the two.

(If you can master that skill and learn to read women well, then you'll actually succeed with both types.)

In my experience, way too many men assume that all women have to be flattered at every turn and that's just not true.

It comes off feeling fake to me. Like I'm with a guy who secretly doesn't believe he should be with me.

I start to wonder what he knows about himself that I don't know. I start to look for his flaws.

Do you compliment your friends all the time? No.

They're your friends. You're equals.

You just hang out with them.

Well, do the same with this woman.

And, broad generalization here, but men tend to give compliments that are looks-based.

When you only comment on a woman's appearance, she's going to start to think that's all you value about her.

And who wants to be with a guy who will leave the minute she gains a few pounds?

Has a health issue?

Or, heaven forbid, gets old?

Valuing someone solely for their appearance will not lead to long-term happiness. Looks fade.

Okay, so it's settled.

You're going to comment on something other than her appearance when you message her.

Great.

Now, and I know *you* won't do this, but I have to say it, just in case.

Please, oh please, oh please, do not refer to her by some sort of looks-oriented name.

What do I mean by this?

No, "Hey, beautiful." Or, "Morning, gorgeous."

You can get away with this once.

But doing so repeatedly? No.

And from the first message? NO.

It says you don't see her as an individual.

Hell, it says you've probably forgotten her name and you just call every woman Baby, Sexy, etc.

Stop it. Stop it right now.

# THE MESSAGE: PART FOUR –
# WATCH YOUR TIMING

This woman needs to believe that you took more than thirty seconds before you decided to message her.

Remember, you're not the douche who's looking for someone to have chat sex with tonight.

You're looking for something lasting. Which means you have time to develop this.

So, do not, under any circumstances, shoot off a quick message to a woman you see is online right now.

What? Why not?

Let me tell you the female experience of this:

She logs into the site to check her messages, update her profile, or look for great guys like you.

And as she's doing whatever it is she came on this site to do, there's a little pop-up box in the bottom corner that's telling her "Rocketboy 123 is checking you out right now!" followed by "Joe1972 is checking you out right now!" Followed by…

You get the picture? These guys are piling up in the corner of her screen.

(Literally on at least one site I know of.)

And then. Then she starts getting messages. "Hey hawtie! Howzit?"

Do you want to put yourself in there with those guys?

No. No, you do not.

So, if you see that she's online, wait to check out her profile. And wait to message her. Give her space.

(This doesn't happen on every site, but it did on the last one I was on and man was it a nightmare. It made me hesitate to go on there at all. I tried different times of day hoping that maybe that would make a difference. It didn't.)

So, what does happen if you just can't stop yourself?

You see her profile, check her out, and shoot off a quick message hoping to catch her attention.

Now what?

Well, first, you probably didn't follow any of the advice above about finding something in her profile to discuss or complimenting her on something other than her photo.

You sent a one-liner. Or a copy and paste. Because you were rushing.

So now she sees your message.

And she thinks, "Wow. Let me see. I logged on two minutes ago. This guy checked me out a minute ago, and now I have a message from him that says *nothing*. Chances that he looked at anything other than my profile picture? None. Odds this is going to go well? Minimal. He's put it all off on me. Next."

Don't do it. Trust me. No woman is such a hot commodity that she's only going to be on this site for a day.

(And if she does drop off the site after a day it's probably because of the sheer number of guys who did exactly what I'm telling you not to do. Remember, *your fellow man is your worst enemy*.)

# THE MESSAGE: PART FIVE –
# SUMMING IT UP

So, what do you say in that first message?

This is easy. You look at her profile, you see something you have in common or that intrigues you, and you write her a message about it.

"Hey, I'm Bill. Saw in your profile that you like to do underwater basket weaving in your spare time. That's so cool. How'd you get into it?"

You also need to give her something to respond to.

(And should do that in all of your messages to her. Many a guy has lost his way by responding to the last message a woman sent without giving her a way to extend the conversation.)

Ask her a question and she may just respond out of politeness, which gives you another chance to impress her.

Send an e-mail that only answers her questions and you have to hope she's interested enough in you to push the conversation forward.

That's why something like this doesn't really work: "Cool profile. Awesome that you like underwater basket weaving."

If she's nice you'll get a "Thanks."

If she's not, or she's stressed by all the other messages she's receiving, she won't respond at all.

That message doesn't invite her to have a conversation with you. It's just a comment.

To her, it says you're probably not interested, but saw her profile and just wanted to say that one thing.

(Because this woman has a lifetime of experience that tells her that if a man is actually interested in her he'll act like he is.)

Okay. So you send her a personal message and play into her sense of politeness by asking a question that requires a response.

DO NOT ask for a date at this stage.

(Unless her profile says that she'd rather just skip this whole exchanging of messages thing and get right to the awkward coffee date.)

She needs to vet you and make sure you aren't a serial killer or some guy with serious anger issues before she meets you in the real world.

(Again, not every woman thinks this way. Some women are sweet and blissfully naïve about the variety of men in this world and assume that a guy who can afford to be online and chatting with her must be a good upstanding citizen.)

(So not true. Even prisoners get computer access. And even doctors can be abusive fucks.)

(But this book isn't for those women and you're not trying to get one of those women, so let's move along.)

Also, if you're funny it should show in your profile, but now would be a good time to show that sense of humor.

No need to force it, though. Just be you.

So, something simple. Something personal. And something that requires a response.

# STEP SEVEN –
# WHAT TO DO IF SHE RESPONDS

She responded! That attractive, compatible woman that you'd love to get to know better actually responded to your message.

Oh man, this is for real.

Congratulations!

Now, *keep your cool*.

This is not the time to send her a message gushing about how beautiful her hair is.

Nor is it the time to get all nervous and confess to her that you were worried she'd never respond to you.

This is the time to take a few breaths, step away from the keyboard, and relax.

Go for a run. Go to a movie.

Do not, under any circumstances, try to start a chat conversation with her.

She responded to one message.

You have a long, long way to go.

Pace yourself.

# COMMUNICATION: PART ONE –
# LET HER BREATHE

I promise, she won't run away.

She messaged you back, so you know she was interested enough (or stupid enough) to be open to dialogue.

In the same way you don't start kissing some woman's neck just because she let you buy her a drink, you don't start spamming some woman because she responded to your message.

Especially if you have a smartphone.

Do this right now: Delete the dating site app from your phone.

I'm serious.

Unless you're just looking for a casual hook-up, having that app on your phone is going to fuck you up.

Delete it.

Here's what happens if you don't:

You're at the grocery store and you're bored. So you check the site.

Oh, look. The woman you like is online. Or she just messaged you.

Well, you have a few minutes, might as well message her back.

Don't.

There will come a time when this works. It is not now.

(The time when this works is when she's just as eager to communicate with you as you are to communicate with her. You'll feel it when this happens. She'll respond almost instantly to your messages. Until that time, play it cool.)

So, why is responding right away such a bad thing? It's just a little message, right?

Wrong.

What would you think of a woman who calls you too much?

You'd think she's needy, maybe? Desperate?

How quickly does "she seemed attractive" turn into "maybe I should check on the rabbit?"

Or, "Damn. I can never go back to my favorite bar because she's there all the time."

So, what do you think a woman is going to think of you if you respond within minutes of her messaging you.

Needy. Desperate. Is he really employed? Does he have anything else going on in his life?

Back away. Limit it to once a day.

Don't wait two weeks or you'll lose her, but don't jump all over her every single time she shows any sign of a positive response.

If you think you've reached that stage where she wants to hear from you more often, now is the time to listen to what she says when she responds.

I tend to give a warning before I drop someone for this because we are in a different day and age and some people have no issue with insta-communication.

So, I might try something non-verbal first.

If a guy responds within five minutes of my last message, I might wait two days to respond. I'm telling him with my actions that he's losing my interest.

(No, I don't sit there and calculate how long I'll make him wait. It's more of a "Ugh. If I write him back right now, he's just going to write me again. Maybe I'll get back to him tomorrow.")

If that doesn't work, I usually say something.

Like, "Wow! You certainly respond quickly. Not going to get fired for always being on your cell phone are you?"

Yes, it is a bit passive-aggressive.

Yes, I could just come out and say, "Dude. Give it a rest, would you?"

But I try subtlety first.

I had one guy who was like this.

I tried to respond at different times of day.

I asked if he had a job since he always responded immediately.

Finally, I just quit responding.

But he followed up.

"Hey, beautiful, haven't heard from you in a few days." (Note: Don't do the beautiful thing…)

I was in a mellow stage and decided to give him another shot.

(See, even I let men get away with these things every once in a while.)

So, I said something like, "Yeah, sorry 'bout that. You wore me out responding to my messages so quickly. Gotta give a girl a little breathing room, you know?"

And what did he do?

Wrote me back in about two minutes.

Do you think I ever responded to him again?

Nope.

Don't do what that guy did.

Listen to what a woman is trying to tell you. Pay attention to how she reacts to what you say.

Give her the space she needs to like you.

Some other guy is not going to steal her from you.

(And if he does, then maybe she wasn't the one for you anyway?)

# COMMUNICATION: PART TWO – LISTEN

We already touched on this before, but let's touch on it again.

The key to success with any woman is to listen to what she's telling you. Verbal and non-verbal.

Sure, there are some general pointers that will help you be more successful with all women.

But, the key to getting *this* particular woman to take an interest in you is to figure out what *she* wants.

Women are not interchangeable. They are not one size fits all.

They don't all value money and prestige. They don't all care about fashion.

You need to figure out what this woman is looking for and tell her how you can provide that.

(No, not in some cheesy job-interview/sales-presentation way.)

But if a woman shows on her profile that she likes to be active and spend time outdoors (by, I don't know mentioning active, outdoorsy hobbies or posting outdoorsy photos) then you talk about how you, too, like to be active and spend time outdoors.

If she's a voracious reader, then you talk to her about books.

If it's true, that is.

(True story. I knew a guy who spent six months grooming a woman he wanted to date because he'd heard how hard to get she was and liked the challenge. He created an entirely false persona to win her—down to the books he liked and classes he took.)

(He succeeded. But that man was a sociopath with no respect for anyone else's feelings. You are not. Don't act like one.)

You also need to figure out what a woman likes or doesn't like when it comes to romantic gestures, because if you get it wrong—too much or too little—you may very well lose your chance.

I was on a site that let you send virtual gifts to people. I found them cheesy and stupid, so no need for anyone to waste their virtual roses on me.

This one guy would send me a virtual gift with *every single message*.

I would respond with something like, "Thank you for the roses, but really, that's not necessary. I'm not much of a gift person."

And he'd keep right on sending them.

I'm pretty sure I finally told him to stop and he still did it. So I quit responding to him.

Because he wasn't listening to me. And if you can't listen at the beginning of a relationship, you certainly aren't going to listen later on.

Another friend of mine was the exact opposite.

(And probably not the type of woman this book is about, but I provide this example to help you understand that you need to know who you are dealing with.)

Her mother raised her to have certain beliefs. One of those beliefs was that she needed to receive a bouquet of roses from her date for any formal dance she attended.

She'd been dating a guy about three months when he invited her to a formal and showed up without flowers.

What happened? She dumped him the next day even though she was madly in love with him.

It took me a week to convince her to forgive him for not knowing what her expectations were.

(Fortunately, when it came time to propose he'd learned his lesson and asked her how big the ring had to be.)

Some women won't care. Some will.

You're best off finding a woman who aligns with how you like to act.

If you like to give gifts, find a woman who likes to receive them.

If you forget every major holiday, including Valentine's Day (even though it's advertised in every window of every store), then find a woman who doesn't care.

Listen to what this woman is saying about what she wants.

Better yet, ask clarifying questions.

No, this is not the, "can I kiss you on the cheek," "can I kiss you on the lips," "can I place my hand…" type of questions.

(Spare me that crap.)

This is the "what kind of restaurant do you prefer for a first date?" type of question.

Do not assume.

Ask. And listen to the answer.

Once again we find ourselves discussing a set of skills that you can use anywhere in life, not just in dating.

Huh. Funny that.

# COMMUNICATION: PART THREE –
# FOCUS ON THE MOMENT

All right. So you're messaging back and forth. Now you need to focus on the moment.

What does that mean?

Focus on the moment? Huh?

It means, keep your conversation focused on *this* woman and *this* relationship.

You're single, right?

So what are you doing talking about your ex? Good relationship, bad relationship, it doesn't matter.

*Don't talk about it.*

If it was a good relationship, you may come off as nostalgic for the past and unable to move forward.

If it was a bad relationship, you're quite likely to come off as bitter or woman-hating. Neither of those are attractive qualities.

(Remember, this is not a woman who goes looking for lost causes in need of an angel to pull them out of the muck. No, she'd very much like for you to be capable of standing on your own two feet, thank you very much.)

So, you have kids. And they matter to you.

Good. Talk about *them*.

Don't talk about how challenging it is to split custody with your ex.

Don't talk about how she's an unstable bitch who you should have never married. Or a whore. Or a money-grubbing....

Get the point?

No?

Let's talk this through.

You think that you're calling one woman a bitch or a whore.

But you're not.

You're telling *this* woman, the one you want to get to know better, the one you hope to date, that when women in your life disappoint you they move from "beautiful" to "bitch."

You're telling her that there's a line somewhere that she might cross that will turn this sweet, affectionate man into someone vile and hateful.

Why would she want to be with someone like that?

If you don't know this, learn it now: There are men out there who *never* call women names like that.

Ever.

Not in the heat of anger. Not when the woman has done terrible things to them.

They never do it.

Understand that what you say about other women matters to the woman you're with.

Even when you say these things because you're trying to flatter her.

I once had a guy say something to me along the lines of "I really like how you're not uptight like most women."

He thought it was flattering.

I thought he was an ass.

Do you think I cared that I was the exception to this man's one-dimensional view of women? Nope.

So keep your conversation current. Avoid the ex talk.

# COMMUNICATION: PART FOUR-
# FOCUS ON THE MOMENT REDUX

Also try to avoid talking about what caused your prior relationships to end.

Because that may not be relevant to the current situation, but she'll think it is.

This seems obvious, right?

But men do it all the time.

True story: I went on a date once with a guy who spent most of the first date complaining that women were always pressuring him to get serious right away when all he wanted was to date around a bit and take things slow.

Nothing wrong with that.

He wanted to keep it casual. I was twenty-three.

Worked for me.

Except he didn't want to keep it casual. Not with me.

So, when I told him I could date a guy like him, but couldn't see myself marrying a guy like him (he had a nine-year-old kid already) he got all pissy even though he'd just spent an hour and a half telling me that he most definitely didn't want to be serious with anyone.

Or what about telling a woman that you split from your last relationship because your ex was pressuring you to settle down and have kids after dating for five years.

Well, unless you're on a date with a woman who has no interest in getting married or having kids, you've just told her that you are not the guy she's looking for.

Maybe the reason that happened in your last relationship wasn't because you have no interest in kids or settling down.

Maybe it was because your ex would have made a shitty mother.

Well, that's not what you just told this woman.

You told this woman that you're commitment phobic. And will string a woman who wants marriage and kids along.

Stay on message.

Sure, a woman wants to know these things. And she'll ask.

But you can always tell her that your prior relationships aren't relevant to the present one and that you'd like to focus on what you're building with her instead of what you had with some other woman who is now part of your past.

(That might work. Chances are you'll have to say something. But if you do, make sure that you don't convey the wrong story when you do it.)

# MAYBE YOU'RE COMING AT THIS WRONG

So, we've covered the basics of finding someone and communicating with them. Follow the above and you probably have a pretty good chance at a date or two.

But maybe that's not what you need.

Maybe you shouldn't even be doing this in the first place.

Two things we need to talk about here:

First, you may not be ready.

Second, she may not be the one.

# YOU MAY NOT BE READY

I hate to say this, but a lot of you are kind of broken and hurt after the end of a relationship.

You're bitter.

You don't know what went wrong.

You're full of anger and sadness.

You have no fucking clue how to fix the issues that led to the demise of your last relationship.

And what do your friends tell you?

"Get out there, man."

"Easiest way to get over the last one is to get under the new one."

"Nothing like a hot twenty-year old to make you forget what's-her-name."

They're wrong.

You are full of some negative shit right now. And that negativity is not going to help you find a good relationship.

It's going to either get you a series of unsatisfying encounters where you wonder what's wrong with all women (and that's a dark path to tread) or you're going to end up with someone who likes to heal men like you.

Now, what happens if you end up with a woman who likes broken men and she fixes you?

That relationship ends and you have to start over again.

Or, more likely, she finds ways to sabotage you so she can continue to take care of you.

Co-dependency. It's some nasty shit.

So, before you jump back in, get some help first.

Go to a counselor. Go to a priest.

Let time work its magic.

But don't do this dating thing until you're ready.

And if you need sex in the meantime, can I direct you back to the *So You're a Douchebag* chapter?

(A man who may not be a douche in general often is one right after a bad breakup. He's kind of an emotionally fucked up asshole for a while.)

Save the quality women for when you're finally ready for something real.

So, that's one kind of guy who just isn't ready.

The other type is the guy who says things like, "all women are stupid bitches" or uses that c word to refer to women on a regular basis.

*That* guy needs to stop dating right now.

He needs to sort his shit when it comes to women. Because he hates them.

And until he can get past that and start to see women as individuals, he is never going to have a satisfying relationship.

How can he love and care for someone if he doesn't see her as his equal?

No man is going to open up enough to be in a real relationship if he thinks all women are just after his money.

Or that they're all manipulative. Or whores.

Or whatever other ridiculous crap certain men spew about women as a blanket group.

And because he can't engage in a relationship the way he should, the relationships he does have are going to reaffirm his negative views.

Turns out that if a man treats a woman like crap it isn't a positive experience for either one of them.

So, if you're that guy, go sort your shit first, okay? For all of us.

This finding love thing is hard enough without people spewing hatred and hurt into the mix.

# SHE MAY NOT BE THE ONE

We went through this whole book assuming that you actually want to get this woman.

Why?

Sure, she has a nice smile. And her profile is original and refreshing compared to everyone else's.

So what?

Let's say you're a nice guy. Kind of shy, kind of quiet.

You don't do well in bar settings. You're a little nervous on dates.

You'd never even think of kissing a girl on a first date. Hell, you're still trying to figure out how to move in for the kiss on date six.

What are you thinking trying to date a woman like this? I'm not saying you can't date an attractive woman. Or even a witty one. Or a smart one.

But this woman is not those women.

This woman is snarky.

She's not afraid to say what she thinks and sometimes it isn't very nice.

She's hard to keep up with.

Do you think that profile is an act?

Do you think she's actually all warm and soft and just put

up a slightly hostile profile for kicks? No.

(Okay, well, maybe just that once...)

No. Chances are she probably toned down her more negative qualities in that profile.

I've dated guys like that. And it's painful. Do you know how bad it feels to have some guy stutter his way through asking you out and know that there is no chance in hell that it's going to work?

I've tried.

When I was younger, I said yes to a few guys like that. It was a disaster.

It's not a matter of being too nice.

If you're a nice guy, don't lose who you are.

It's that nice guys sometimes try to date women who aren't nice. At least, not in the same way.

I have said it before, I will say it again:

Look past the smile.

Look past the eyes.

And the hair. And the curves.

Read what the woman is saying. *Really* read it.

And ask yourself if that's the kind of woman you want to deal with every single day.

Now maybe you're not the nice guy.

Maybe you're the asshole.

The guy who says, "get over yourself" every time a woman gets angry.

You see that profile and you don't give a shit how snarky the woman is because she's hot and you don't take crap from anyone.

Stop. Walk away.

Because you know what you're about to do?

Where a nice guy tries to pat the fire out with his bare hands and ends up burned, you're going to throw gasoline on the situation and turn it into a wildfire.

Is that how you want to live your life?

Is that the relationship you want to come home to?

Why do that to yourself? Or her?

If you know you're just going to be an ass when this woman's angry, then walk away. Find someone you care enough about to help.

Maybe you're neither of those guys.

She still may not be the one for you.

Ask yourself—what type of woman will make you happy?

Will this woman improve your life?

If yes, then contact her.

If not, then don't

And remember, you cannot tell the type of person from the photo. You can't.

(You can tell a *lot* from a photo, but the wrong parts of your mind are working when you're looking at that photo, so you need to focus on the words first.)

Look at what she's saying.

She's putting her best foot forward (or the best foot forward that she cares to put forward).

If you can already see warning signs, seriously reconsider getting to know this woman better.

There are other women out there. Better women.

I know it doesn't feel like that at times, but there really are.

Don't compromise. It'll make you miserable.

# SUMMING IT UP

It's easy with dating (online in particular) to focus on the physical. To see a pretty smile and think you've found the woman for you.

Don't do that.

Looks don't mean everything.

You need to know if you're compatible with this woman first.

And you have a wealth of information available. So use it.

What does this woman want? What does she like?

Maybe what she said is complete bullshit, but it's what she chose to tell you. Pay attention.

And be honest with yourself. Is this really the kind of person you want to be with?

Don't choose someone you'd have to contort yourself to match.

Choose someone you can be yourself with.

And once you've found someone like that, approach her with confidence.

Because, whatever your flaws and limitations, you also have strengths. And it's those strengths that make you worthy of this woman.

Do it in a way that makes it clear that you're interested in her.

Her. Not just any woman. *This* woman.

Do it in a way that shows her that you're a quality guy. That you like women.

Be her equal.

Remember that you're a complete stranger to this woman, so take it slow and give her the space to like you back.

Do all this and you know what? You'll be ahead of 95% of the guys out there.

(And you may even find yourself doing better at work, too. Because a lot of this shit applies as much to work as to dating.)

# POSTSCRIPT:
# THIS THING CALLED THE REAL WORLD

Online dating isn't for everyone.

There's this thing called the real world where you can go and do the things you love to do and find other people who love to do those same things and form a connection with them.

One of those people might even be a woman that you can date. Or you might meet guys who know women you can date.

It's crazy how that works.

(Happens all the time, though. And should probably happen more.)

Online dating is an easy out.

You can hide behind a keyboard and pretend that you're making progress towards meeting someone when you're not.

And it works for some people. It really does.

But for others it can be a terrible choice.

So, if you've tried it and you're not finding what you're looking for, step away from the computer.

Pursue your passions, whatever they may be.

Do what you love and look for people who love it, too.

Oh, and when you meet someone interesting, stop.

Hold back. Get to know them through the activity.

Don't be that guy who hovers around a woman to get her attention.

Do your thing. Smile occasionally and be friendly, but be confident enough to let something develop.

Trust me. If she's interested, you'll see the signs.

(Hint: If she always seems to be around, you're doing well.)

(Either that or you have a really attractive best friend that she likes.)

Let her signal her interest and *then* you can ask her out. Not before.

Some people are an acquired taste. Give her the time to acquire it.

# WHAT IF IT STILL ISN'T ENOUGH?

I let a buddy of mine read this book and he said something about how he'd done all these things and still struck out.

But he hadn't really.

I've known him for ten years and he's had plenty of dates from online dating.

What he didn't find were satisfying relationships.

(He's finally in one now, but it took a long time.)

Whether he'll admit it or not, his main issue was that he focused too much on appearance.

He went through a lot of heartache because he kept looking for women who were 8's or 9's and ignoring their issues.

And he'd stick in there with each one far longer than he should've because he was a decent guy who wanted a real relationship.

Look, the advice in this book is not going to find you love.

But if you follow it, you should at least make it to a first date with that woman who interests you.

And from there? Keep doing the same.

Listen to her. Respect her.

Only continue the relationship if she's improving your life and you're improving hers.

Look past her appearance to who she really is.

Pay attention to what she's telling you and decide whether that's who you want to be with.

It'll happen someday. It will. You just have to keep trying and get out of your own way.

Hopefully this book has given you a few tips on how to do that.

(And, if not, hopefully it's given you a few good laughs.)

Good luck!

# You Have A Date, Don't F It Up

## CASSIE LEIGH

# CONTENTS

# INTRODUCTION

Well, it's that time again. Time to knock you upside the head about silly dating mistakes that might be costing you that chance at ever-lasting love and happiness. Or, if nothing else, another date.

This book is for those who've mastered (or think they have) the first step of dating—getting a woman to agree to go out with you—and are now trying to figure out how to get from "yes, I'll go out with you" to the actual date and from that first date to a second and from a second to a third.

Beyond that point any advice—other than be a nice person and listen to the woman you're dating and give her what she wants—starts to fall apart.

(This goes without saying, but you should also be getting what you want out of the relationship, too. And if you can't get enough of what you want while giving her enough of what she wants, it's not going to work.)

Anyway. Back to the point of this book.

While my other books have focused on online dating, this book should apply to any sort of dating. There are definitely differences between going on a first date with someone you've only met online versus going on a date with someone you've actually met in real life, but most of the principles we'll talk about apply to both.

As I've said in my other books, I can't speak for all women, I can only speak for myself. Why one particular date you went on didn't work will have to remain one of life's eternal mysteries. What I can do is give you some insights based on my own personal experiences and reactions.

And since I'm one of the pickiest, most judgmental people I know when it comes to dating—not that most men realize this, which is part of what you need to understand about women—if you can make it past my deal-breakers you should be golden with most women.

Can I guarantee that you'll be successful with *all* women after you read this book? No. And you shouldn't want that. Because some people just aren't compatible and it's fine to acknowledge that and move on to better prospects. (Even if she's really attractive.)

Hopefully after reading this book you'll be able to fix the basic mistakes a lot of men make that lose them that chance of dating someone wonderful for them. By the time you're done, you should be able to (a) make it to the actual date, (b) have a good enough time that there's a second one if you're interested and interesting to her, and (c) maybe even make it to the next date after that. Beyond that point, whether things continue forward or not will very much be a matter of you and the individual woman you're dating.

One last thing before we get started: As stated in my other books, I'm writing this book for men interested in dating women. If you're a man looking for men, some of what I say here is probably applicable, but a lot won't be. Same for a woman looking for men or women.

So, this book is for men wanting to date women and not doing as well as they'd like.

# DOES THIS SOUND FAMILIAR?

You meet a woman you like. She's attractive and interesting and you guys seem to hit it off, so you ask her out. And she say yes. Congratulations! You have a date with a woman you'd like to see more of.

But…

When you try to call her, she doesn't answer. (Or you find out she gave you a fake number.)

Or if she does answer, she blows you off before you can talk.

Or when you try to make plans to get together, she's constantly busy.

Or she agrees to get together, but somewhere in between agreeing to get together and actually setting up firm plans, she bails on you. Maybe she says she's just too busy right now. Maybe she just stops responding.

Maybe you do make plans and she stands you up.

Or cuts out before the date has really begun.

Or you guys have what seems like a great first date and then…nothing. You never hear from her again.

I'll admit it. I'm guilty of all of the above except standing a guy up and cutting out early once a date starts. (Those two I think are rude, so if I have firm plans with a guy I'll go on the date and suffer through it no matter how miserable. Or I'll be decent enough to cancel in advance.)

But all of the rest?

Yep. Done that. More than once.

Why? Why do women say they'll go out with you and then bail? (Men do this, too, by the way. This isn't isolated to women. But for this book we'll focus on women and why they do these things and how you can avoid having it happen to you as often as it may be happening now.)

What went wrong?

How did you go from a woman who seemed interested to radio silence?

Or, worse, a woman who actually met up with you and seemed to have a good time to a woman who never took your calls again?

Well, let's start at the beginning, shall we?

# FIRST, DID SHE ACTUALLY AGREE TO GO OUT WITH YOU?

Ah, weren't expecting that were you? You figured that if you asked a woman for her number and she gave it to you that that actually meant something.

Nope. Doesn't mean a thing.

I am not proud of this, but, especially when I was younger, I would give my number to men who asked for it with no intent of ever speaking to them again. (Or, in the pre-cellphone days, I'd say I couldn't give out my number because my dad didn't like me to—which was actually true because I wasn't capable of giving a fake number and he had to screen the calls—and I would take men's numbers instead and then I'd never call.)

Why?

Why do women do this?

Honest answer: Because it's much easier than the alternative, which is to tell some perfectly nice guy that even though I barely know him I already know I'm not interested.

I mean, what am I supposed to say? "Um, you know, I'm really just not that into men with beards."

Or, true example, "While it's great that you flunked out of community college five times and now work as a parking lot attendant that's just not the kind of guy I picture myself with."

Instead, I say sure, take the number and move on with my life without some ugly scene. Because I've learned through more than one unpleasant encounter that saying no results in one of two outcomes, both of which I don't want to deal with.

In the first scenario the guy asks, "Why not?"

This can either be a perfectly legitimate question asked by a nice, decent guy. Like, "Hey, I thought we were getting along, why wouldn't you want to see me again?"

Or it can be asked as a defensive, "What the hell? I thought we were cool" sort of question.

Whichever tone the guy takes, it's not fun to have to explain to someone that they just didn't spark things enough for you to want to keep it going. And sometimes the reason a guy isn't interesting is something you don't want to share. You know like, "I can't stop staring at your unibrow and it really just bugs the shit out of me."

(At which point the guy says, "I could shave it, it's not that big a deal" but I'm thinking, "But you're still the type of guy who didn't even realize that having a bushy unibrow would be a turn-off to a lot of women. And what else do I not see right now that's going to be like that? And, seriously, you're just willing to change on a dime for a woman you just met so she'll go out with you? Have some pride, man. Stand up for your beliefs and find a woman who loves her a sexy unibrow-wearing crazy man.")

Anyway. It's not a conversation anyone wants to have. I don't live to hurt others' feelings and, believe it or not, screening a guy's call is a lot less painful than any in-person critique I could give. By giving him my number and then screening his calls, he gets to make up some great ego-saving reason I didn't answer. Maybe my ex called and we got back together. Maybe I was too drunk and forgot I'd given out my number and it's nothing personal that I'm not answering. Maybe...whatever. *Anything* is better than the truth.

But the real reason I don't like to give the flat-out rejection is the other way this can go down. I say, "No, I don't think so" or in some other way reject a guy and I get, "Whatever. Not like you're that hot anyway." Or "Whatever, bitch." Or any variation on "I wasn't really interested in you and you're ugly, stupid, and/or dumb."

Seriously. Happens to every woman at some point.

Some guy who a minute before wanted to spend more time with her is suddenly insulting and rude and telling her how he wouldn't hook up with her if she was the last woman on earth and how he was just trying to do some charity work or…

Whatever. Fragile little ego that can't handle rejection.

Sadly it's happened often enough to me and my friends over the years that it isn't even a surprise. (And, no, I'm not the type to pretend I like a guy to get him to buy me drinks or to in any way lead him on if I'm not interested. I will talk to a man who approaches me, but half the time I'm batting away any sort of flirtatious comments or attempts to touch me, so this is not some situation where I gave the guy the wrong impression unless you think I did that by acknowledging that he existed.)

Now, granted, this scenario often happens much earlier in the conversation (why men think a woman walking down the street has nothing better to do than stop and let them chat her up, I will never know), but it can happen at any point if the guy is that kind of guy.

Fortunately, scenario number two happens less often now that I'm older, uglier, and bitchier, but it still does happen. You would be genuinely surprised by the number of men who go from wanting to sleep with a woman to calling her names in the space of thirty seconds. Like the fact that she isn't willing to hook up with them is some sort of personal attack and affront to their ego.

Don't be that guy, by the way.

A woman doesn't want to give you her number? Move on. She doesn't want to talk to you? Move on. There are other, better women for you out there. Spend your time and energy finding them.

Also, now is a good time to remind you that your biggest enemy in finding a woman to date or marry or whatever you're looking for, is your fellow man. Because *you* may be great. You may be interesting and relatively attractive and worth her checking out. But you have to get through all the bullshit other men have thrown at her to get her to see that. And if you do anything to remind her of those creepers she's had to deal with in the past—like call her a name or treat her like a game to be won—you're done. She'll move on.

So anyway. Back to the point. Just because some woman gave you her number, doesn't mean she actually wants to see you again. Sad, but true.

# ENTER THE BOYFRIEND

This is also the stage when a mysterious boyfriend can suddenly appear. You try to talk to a woman and she says, "Sorry, I have a boyfriend."

Or you're having a great conversation with a woman, you ask for her number, and she says, "Sorry, but my boyfriend doesn't like me to give out my number to strange guys."

Or you get her number or her agreement to go out sometime but when you follow-up she suddenly drops a boyfriend into the conversation like she didn't understand that you were asking her on a date, not trying to be her friend.

Does she have a boyfriend?

Maybe. But probably not.

(Ironic that women tend to make up boyfriends in these scenarios whereas a lot of men seem to forget they have a girlfriend in the same scenario, which is maybe why it works so well.)

The fake boyfriend is one of my go-to excuses for not engaging with a guy who's showing interest when I'm not feeling it. Or for backing out of getting together with someone I've changed my mind about. Especially if it's someone I don't know well but can expect to see again, like someone who hits on me at work.

I'll give you an example. Many, many years ago I worked at a bookstore. A guy who worked somewhere in the mall came in and we talked a little. I helped him find whatever book he was looking for and was nice and sweet, which I generally am to strangers, especially at work.

The next day he came back, hovered around nervously for quite some time, and finally got up the urge to ask if I'd like to maybe get a water or something sometime.

(Side note: First, if you want to ask a woman out, don't hover. Just do it. Hovering won't make her more likely to say yes, but it might make her say no if she notices that you're doing it, which I usually do. Also, unless there's some cool ironic joke you two have going on about drinking water, don't ask a woman out for a water. Even if that's all *you* drink, don't ask her out for a water. Ask her out for a coffee and when you get there order your water and let her order whatever it is she drinks.)

So there I was at work, knowing I'd see the guy around.

I didn't want to hurt his feelings, because he was one of those quiet shy types who took ten minutes building up his courage. But I also knew he was not going to be a good fit for me.

(Another side note: Most men who meet me in real life think that I'm very nice. And I am in many ways. Especially to the shy, awkward types. I'm not going to be rude or insulting to a guy like that. I will smile and talk about whatever they want to talk about and make the situation as comfortable as possible for both of us while it lasts. But I *know* that a man like that will not do well with me. Because when I'm angry, men like that want to make it better. But what they need to do is get out of my way until I get over myself. So I don't date those types. It's too cruel to put them through that.)

Anyway. He asked me out. And, not wanting to just reject him, I said, "yeah, sure, but I really can't talk right now" hoping that non-committal response and blow-off would end things.

It didn't. He was back the next day asking when my break was. Enter the boyfriend.

I said I really couldn't do anything that day because I'd been up late the night before talking to my boyfriend who was going to school on the East coast and it had made me late for work, so I was skipping my break to make up for it.

He fled. And I never saw him again.

I felt horrible. But...It did save me from the whole, "you are not a good fit for me" conversation.

That was not the first time I'd manufactured a boyfriend and it wasn't the last. It works, because most men will back off if they hear a woman is in a relationship. (Not all, though. There's the "Well we can just be friends" guys who are either smooth enough to know it can be a lie or who think they can charm a woman away from any man if given the opportunity. But that kind of guy is easy to straight up reject because he rarely takes it personally and he's on to the next woman within minutes.)

So what do you do if she suddenly mentions a boyfriend?

Nothing.

Move on to someone who is actually interested in dating you. Same goes for a woman who is suddenly so busy with work or friends that she just can't possibly fit you into her schedule anytime soon.

True or not, it doesn't matter. She isn't interested enough to bother with. And no woman is so amazing and wonderful and perfect that you need to waste your time trying to push through that. Just move on.

# BEFORE YOU GET TOO DISCOURAGED...

By now you should realize that women often (and this is more for in-person conversations than online dating) will say yes to going on a date when they don't really mean yes.

But sometimes it goes the other way.

Sometimes a woman does want to go out with you but she genuinely is busy, or she does give you the wrong number by accident, or your email gets sent to her spam folder and she never even knows you reached out.

A good friend of mine has been dating a woman for a couple of years now, but when they first met she told him she couldn't get together for a couple of weeks because things at work were really busy. It wasn't that she wasn't interested. It just so happened she had a two-week work trip planned and couldn't squeeze time out of the couple of days she had free before the trip.

He could've written her off and assumed she really just didn't want to see him. But by hanging in there and playing it cool, he's now in a very happy relationship.

So don't get too cynical about all of this.

Just don't pin your hopes on one woman this early in the game. Keep looking around and be open to meeting someone else.

And with the woman who seems to be blowing you off? Try once, try twice, and then move on. If she circles back your way a little bit later and you don't have anything better in the works, give her another chance.

(Or not. There is nothing wrong with knowing how you want to be treated and only dealing with people who treat you that way. I recently had a guy cancel plans with me because he's too busy at work. Personally, that was a deal-breaker. I'm not interested in dating a man who lives for his work. And, quite frankly, I think the work excuse is usually code for "I'm just not that into you.")

Anyway. Don't always assume that because she didn't jump all over you or because something went wrong that she isn't interested.

Let me give you an example.

A while back I went out to meet some college friends for drinks. A buddy of one of the guys I knew dropped by and joined us. He ended up sitting next to me and we flirted back and forth for a couple hours. When it was time to leave, he offered to give me a ride home. I said sure. He drove me home.

When we pulled up outside my place, he said, "We should get together sometime."

And I said, "Yeah, sure, I'd like that," and then I got out of the car and went inside.

Sounds good, right?

One little problem.

The guy didn't have my number. Now, if I'd been really, really interested in him I would've probably nailed him down on some details of when/where this was going to happen (like, "Yeah, sure. Have you seen the latest Jason Statham movie? Because I'm dying to see it.") Or at least I would have made sure he had my number in his phone before I got out of the car.

But, even though I'd done the "yeah, sure" thing and left before he could get my number, he wasn't down for the count at that point. He'd just run into twenty-plus years' worth of ingrained instinct. At this point in my life, shrugging guys off is something I do without even thinking about it.

(If I actually like a guy, I have to fight myself to not do that. And I often have to give it a bit of thought and then come back to him later, because my immediate reaction is almost always "just leave me alone, please.")

Where he "failed" is in not following up with our mutual friend to get my number. Or, better yet, emailing me, because we'd both been part of an email chain where we all arranged to meet up.

Of course, I could've done the same thing. I had his email, too. But I didn't. Because I wasn't *that* interested in him.

But don't assume it's over just because of something like that. If you're really interested and you have a way to do so without being creepy (we'll touch on that later), give it another try to make sure it wasn't a simple miscommunication.

# WHAT IF SHE DOES ACTUALLY SEEM INTERESTED?

So let's say you got her number and she actually answered when you called or texted. Or you messaged her about going out and she said she'd like that.

Are you free and clear now? Is this going to result in a date? Oh, hell no.

You are in the no-date-yet danger zone. Now you have to successfully negotiate all the details of a date without losing her. This is a point where things can go wrong fast.

You'd think it isn't a big deal. All you have to agree to is where to get together and when. How hard can that be?

You'd be surprised.

There are sooo many ways things can fall apart at this point, it isn't even funny.

But first let's take a moment to remind you of something I discussed in the other books that we haven't touched on yet: Women are not some one-size-fits-all sort of Barbie doll. There are no clear-cut rules you can apply to all women in all situations. Some women will like a man who takes charge and knows what he wants. (Like me.) Some would find that kind of guy overbearing and obnoxious. (Also sometimes me. Ha!)

So. Even though we're going to talk about how things can fall apart at this stage, keep in mind that if you know this woman better than I do and don't think what I'm saying here makes sense for dealing with her, then don't do it. Follow your gut.

If she's very particular about things and willing to communicate that to you, listen and follow her direction. But if you don't have a good read on her yet? Or think she's the kind to agree to plans without much fuss? Then follow the approach I'm about to recommend.

Also, before we begin, keep in mind there's a bit of a ticking clock between when a woman agrees to go out with you and when that date needs to happen. Personally, unless there are some very good reasons for it—like one of you is out of the country or the state—I wouldn't allow more than a week to pass between suggesting a date and actually having it.

Why? Well, first, she could meet someone else, go out with them, and like them enough to no longer be interested in you. Second, it gets tricky to keep up the momentum of the conversation when you can't get together. And, third, if you don't make it a priority to see her, you're not signaling to her that you're genuinely interested. What you're doing is showing her that there are a lot of things in your life more important than going out with her.

It's possible she's the reason for the delay. In which case you should ask yourself how interested she is in you? And is it worth holding out for a woman who puts that many things before you? Because you need to value yourself if you legitimately want to find long-term happiness.

I know too many men willing to settle for less than they deserve because (a) the woman is really attractive and they let that blind them to how miserably she treats them or (b) they're so worried about being alone that they'll settle for anything they can get.

Don't do that to yourself.

Whatever you look like, whatever you do for a job, whatever your interests are, there is a woman out there who will make you happy and be glad to be with you. Find her. And don't settle until you do.

Alright, enough of that.

So you're interested and she's interested, and now all you have to do is agree on the particulars and not f up between here and the actual date.

Let's spend a couple chapters discussing where you can potentially go wrong at this point and some strategies to get past them.

# WHERE AND WHEN TO MEET

Believe it or not, things can completely derail over an inability to agree on where and when to meet. If you think about it, it's actually a negotiation. You two have to work together to determine what you're going to do, where you're going to do it, and when. And that isn't always easy.

Now, I understand that this is a first date and you want to be somewhat accommodating to your date's interests. I get that. But I would recommend that the best approach here is to take charge.

By that I mean, you say something like this: "What do you say to going to [insert thing you guys talked about and you know she's interested in]. I'm free Saturday, if that works for you."

If she likes your idea and is also free Saturday, you're 90% of the way there in one message. All she has to do is say, "Sounds great! Want to meet at noon in the south parking lot?"

Of course, it rarely goes that smoothly.

Instead she'll say "Sounds great," and then you'll have to suggest when to meet and will probably forget to suggest where and there'll be a good five emails exchanged before you've nailed down the details. But it's still better than the alternative.

The alternative goes something like this:

You: "So what do you want to do? Dinner maybe? Or we could go to that exhibit you mentioned."

Her: "Yeah, dinner sounds good. Where were you thinking?"

You: "What about Hennesy's?"

Her: "Which one?"

You: "The one on 16th and Blake."

Her: "Oh, yeah. That works."

You: "Great. How about Friday?"

Her: "Sure. What time?"

You: "Six?"

Her: "I can't do that early. How about seven?"

You: "Okay."

And that's assuming you immediately agreed on what, when, and where. Look at that conversation again. Do you see how many times you gave her a chance to end the conversation? Or for the conversation to derail?

Think about how this plays out if you're both busy people who aren't constantly connected to your phone/computer/ whatever so there's a delay between each message. That string of texts or emails could take three days. And if it takes too long you run into the situation where you're trying to make plans for the next day which is generally a no-no.

The vague approach allows too much room for one or the other of you to think things have gone wrong or that you're being ignored or that the other person isn't really that interested or for you to make some side comment that ends things completely.

That's why suggesting what, where, and when in the first message is a better approach. The shorter the distance between her saying yes and the actual date, the better.

But, because you don't know her well and this is a first date, you should still remain flexible. If she comes back and says, "I really don't like Thai, but I'd be up for Mexican," great. Suggest a specific Mexican place.

But in every single message, be trying to lock down the details and close the deal. Vague "sure, maybe, whatever" communication will never get you where you want to go, which is on an actual date.

# AN ASIDE: THE RULES BEHIND
## SETTING UP A DATE

So there's this book called *The Rules* and some of the advice in there has maybe trickled down into women's subconscious. It isn't so much playing games as wanting to be respected and knowing that certain times mean more than others and that agreeing to go on a date with almost no notice conveys a certain message.

I've never read the book and I'm not even sure all the little rules I carry around in my head originated there, but I'll give you a brief rundown of the ones I seem to apply without realizing it.

- A dinner date is "more serious" than a lunch date
- A breakfast date is not something you do on as a first date
- A date for a Friday night or a Saturday night is "more serious" than a date for any other night of the week
- A date involving a meal is "more serious" than a date involving drinks, even if that drink date evolves into a date that includes a meal
- Dinner and a movie is a sort of standard clichéd date, but rare these days in my experience

- Early dates should not involve other family members
- Early dates should also not involve friends
- You generally shouldn't ask or agree to go on a date with only a day's notice. (It implies you have no life or are willing to cancel existing plans for this person.)
- If you're older than about twenty, no date should involve a fast food restaurant.
- A man who chooses some incredibly expensive restaurant for a first date is trying too hard.
- Chain restaurants are best avoided, but seem to be a far too common choice.

Those are the ones I can think of off the top of my head. If you look at them you can see where you might get into trouble. You ask a woman on Thursday if she wants to meet you for dinner on Friday and you're not only asking for prime date real estate (dinner on a Friday), you're also asking her to agree to a date with almost no notice.

If I recall what I've heard correctly, if you want a date for a weekend, you should have plans made by Wednesday at the absolute latest. Now, does this mean she won't agree to a Friday date if you ask on Thursday? No. I think I've done it. But there is this little calculus she does in her head when you do that and it involves how interesting you are, how much she cares about perception, etc.

And you really do need to finalize the date a day or two in advance. I recently went through a scenario where on a Friday morning we had discussed meeting on a Sunday and then the guy didn't get back to me on Friday afternoon or Saturday. By the time I woke up Sunday, he wasn't part of my plans for the day, because I'm not going to sit around on the off chance that this guy who couldn't finalize plans is going to come through at the last minute. Nope.

(Turns out in that case that he thought he'd sent an email but he hadn't and we didn't resolve the miscommunication until Monday when he followed up. Unfortunate, but didn't prevent me from mentally writing him off by the time Sunday rolled around.)

So, when suggesting a date, keep the above in mind. She's more likely to agree to a date that you set up a few days in advance that is less serious. So, afternoon coffee on a Sunday that you schedule by Thursday is more likely to get a yes than a fancy dinner on Friday that you try to schedule on Thursday.

# DON'T SAY STUPID SHIT

Alright. Back to ways you can mess things up before the actual date.

Even though this woman has agreed to go out on a date with you, that doesn't mean she will. Especially if you slip up and say something really stupid or offensive to her before the actual date.

Unless you're frickin' gorgeous and accomplished and a man any woman would kill to be with (which makes me wonder why you're reading this) a woman will walk away if you offend her or say something that makes her realize you are not someone she wants to waste time on.

(Well, at least I will.)

I'll give you an example.

Now, granted, this guy already had a strike against him for lying about his age on his profile, but I had still agreed to go out with him. So we were doing the back and forth about where to meet up. He went with the, "Hey, where do you think you'd want to meet? Somewhere down south maybe?" approach.

And then we exchanged email after email after email with nothing decided. Keep in mind here, that I try to be very flexible at this stage and let the man "take charge" and choose the actual place. So, I said something like, "That works for me. Where were you thinking?" etc. etc.

But we kept going back and forth and not settling on plans.

This went on for a few days until finally I said something like, "How about we meet at X restaurant on such-and-such street at 6 on Wednesday?"

To which he responded, "Wow. I can see why that guy thought you were a dominatrix."

Really?

I try to finalize plans and suddenly I'm some whip-wielding woman in latex?

Now, a little context here. When I'd first joined this particular dating site some guy had messaged me about how he was looking for an older woman to take a firm hand with him. (I kid you not.) So I'd had a little back and forth with this guy I was trying to arrange a date with about that happening in a "you wouldn't believe what women have to deal with on here" sort of way.

His little comment about me being a dominatrix was not funny. Because it came off as a "back in your place" sort of comment. Like my trying to finalize plans was in some way offensive.

Not the kind of guy I was going to waste more time on.

I mean, seriously. You want to insult me before we've ever even met? No. I'll stay at home and watch Luke Cage with my pup rather than waste two hours of my life with you, thank you very much.

So don't get cute. And don't say stupid shit. It's too hard to fix when you're not face-to-face.

If you wouldn't make that kind of joke or comment on a job interview, don't make it online or via text while trying to set up a date. What you think you said and the tone you think you said it in, may not be how it comes across. Put your best foot forward until you're together in person and you can read her reactions.

# DON'T GET COMFY

Another reason I recommend moving from asking for a date to the actual date in less than a week is because it doesn't let you slip up and get too comfortable. Honestly, with online dating, I think you need to move from match to date within about two weeks if you can. Even faster than that if possible.

Especially if you've just ended a long-term relationship. It's far too easy to fall back into your old patterns from your relationship and get too comfortable with this woman before you should be.

Honestly, and it sounds stupid, the more you treat this like a potential job interview, the better off you'll be. It'll remind you that your goal right now is to impress her enough to get the "offer." In this case, the date.

Let's walk through a few real-world examples from my oh-so-wonderful dating past where guys got a little too comfy too soon.

The first couple come from a point in time a few years back when I was living in New Zealand but moving back to the States. During the last month I was in New Zealand I figured I'd get a head start on things by opening an online dating account in the States, so that when I returned I'd have someone to go out with right away.

(Not recommended. Too long of a time lag between

matching with someone and seeing them in person as you're about to see.)

So I met a couple of guys who showed some promise. And, because I wasn't there to meet up with them, we kept exchanging messages over the course of that month.

The first guy slowly moved from suggesting that we go out when I was back in town, to suggesting that we have our first date at his house, to talking about how that date could be in his basement snuggled up on the couch watching movies.

Think about this for a second. A guy I had never met before in person, who as far as I knew could be a serial killer, wanted me to come to his house and hang out in his basement.

No.

No, no, no.

Way too intimate for a first date.

And, honestly, unless you're trying to set up a date with your best friend's sister or someone equivalent, you need to keep in mind that you don't know this woman either. You don't want her to know where you live yet. Not until you've determined she isn't going to cut up your bunny rabbit and leave it cooking on the stove. (That's from a Glenn Close movie for those of you too young to remember...)

Because this guy got way too comfy too fast, I went from being willing to meet him for a coffee to never wanting to see him in real life, ever, ever, ever. (There were a few other little red flags there, too, but that was the final straw for me.) I'm sure he spent too much time reading my messages and looking at my photos and thought he knew me. He didn't.

The second guy got too comfortable in a different way. He started talking about things you just don't tell someone you're not in a relationship with. Like how he'd played softball the day before and his shoulder was really hurting him and he'd had to ice it and put Bengay on and how now that he was older he found that he just didn't get around as well anymore and...

Do you think that's sexy? Or appealing in any way? Do you think talking about your aches and pains will make a woman like you more?

It won't. I mean, sure, that's your life, but maybe don't share that before the first date?

Remember, think job interview. Would you tell a prospective employer about your aches and pains? No. No you would not.

A friend of mine, who is a little less rigorous about screening out the crazies (and actually willing to share her phone number and personal email before meeting someone in person which I will not do if I can avoid it), had a few more examples of men who got too comfy too soon.

One guy texted her "Good morning, Beautiful" every single morning leading up to their date.

They'd never met in person. Never had a date.

Maybe he thought it was sweet. Or cute.

It wasn't.

That right there is downright creepy. Don't do that.

Remember, until you meet this woman in person you're just a weird stranger on the internet or some dude who hit on her at the bar. You could be anyone. All of your pictures and likes and dislikes could be complete fabrications.

(I think my friend actually went on that date, but I wouldn't have, because that would've been a sign to me of a potential crazy stalker type and I don't go there if I can avoid it. Been there, done that.)

The other one that was a way-too-soon thing was the guy who sent her a Facebook friend request. He didn't ask if he could do it or talk to her about it beforehand either. He just used her email to track her down on Facebook and then let her know he'd done so by sending the friend request. (The reason the email I use for dating is not an email I use for anything else.)

Now, this could just be a generational thing. I'm sure there are many twenty-something women out there who wouldn't bat an eye at it, but I certainly do.

I say far too much shit on Facebook for me to be friends with just anyone. Also, first dates sometimes don't go well and I really don't need some guy I don't want to see again being my Facebook friend.

So hold off until at least the second date on that. Perhaps even longer.

I have another friend who is now happily married with twins, who dated her now-husband for at least nine months before they became FB friends. And it's a good thing, too. He didn't need to know that she'd posted about freezing her eggs or about the dude she'd hit on at the gym a few weeks before she met him. And maybe she didn't need to see whatever dumbass posts he'd made the year before.

They are very happy now, but that might not have happened if they'd had full access to each other's' FB posts from day one. So, chill out a bit.

And remember: No matter how great the conversations have been, don't let yourself get too comfortable. At least not until you get that first date under your belt. Remind yourself that you are strangers and that you want to impress her at this stage.

# KEEP YOUR COOL

Let's say you somehow snagged the number of a woman you think is way out of your league. And you are on cloud 9. You just can't get over how amazingly lucky you are to have a shot at this woman. I mean, she's gorgeous. And she gave you her number and even answered the phone when you called.

You cannot let her know this.

You need to keep your cool. Do not show her how much out of your league you think she is.

No gushing.

No over the top ridiculousness.

The following is a true story even though it doesn't seem like it should be.

Back in college I was walking through the main quad one day and some guy stopped me to tell me how much he liked my arms. (As you might have figured out by now, men say weird things to women all the time. Or at least they do to me.)

Anyway. I was in a good mood so I talked to him. And when he asked for my number, I gave it to him.

He gave me his as well. Written on, I believe, a five-dollar bill. That should've been a huge red flag, but sadly, it wasn't the first time a man had written his number on money and given it to me. Still. (Don't do that, BTW. It's weird and she's far more likely to spend the money than keep it.)

Anyway. Good mood. Gave him my number. Got his. He called. I answered.

And we proceeded to have one of the most bizarre conversations I have ever had in my life. It seems he worked for a jewelry importer, so he told me that instead of bringing me roses for our first date he was going to bring me jewelry. And somewhere in that conversation he also told me he'd let me drive his car. And that when I went home for the summer from college he'd buy me a fax machine so we could keep in touch. (This was a long time ago. Cellphones existed but they were about three times the size of your hand and weighed a good five pounds.) I think he also mentioned flying me to Bangladesh to meet his family. It was either on that call or the next time he called.

I quickly moved from somewhat amused to "oh hell no."

This guy was way too over the top.

And when I tried to point out all the reasons we weren't compatible—I deliberately chose the opposite interests in everything from music to movies—he didn't care. He just thought I was really beautiful and that's all that mattered to him.

Don't do this. Don't even do a toned-down version of this.

Play it cool. If the woman is the right one for you, you do not need to bribe her or buy her or do ridiculous things to impress her. You should approach any woman you want to date as if you're an equal and you deserve her time and attention. Make her believe that you will improve her life by being in it. You do that by being confident in who you are and what you bring to the table.

So none of this desperate over-the-top stuff. Keep your cool.

Now, maybe you disagree with me on this. You have lots of money and you know that's your main source of appeal for women.

Okay.

You might want to work on that, by the way. Even if she sticks around long enough to marry you she'll probably divorce you at some point if that's all you bring to the table.

But let's talk this through.

Money *can be* an endearing quality to some women. But you don't have to be ridiculous about it. And if you are going to be flashing your cash to appeal to women, you need to make sure you're dealing with the type of woman who cares about that.

I'm not that woman. My alarm bells start going off the moment a man leans too heavily on how much he makes or has without offering anything else.

Other women are different. They love the thought of a man spending hundreds or thousands of dollars on them when he barely knows them.

But until you know what kind of woman you're dealing with? Hold back a bit.

Also, keep in mind that a woman whose interest can essentially be bought with money is a woman who can be lost to a man with more money. And know that if you're with a woman like that and you hit a downturn financially you will not only be broke you will also be alone.

Those types of relationships do work, so if that's how you want to play it more power to you, just know that leaning too heavily on how much you make can drive away women who are looking for more substance than that.

And, no matter what, with any woman, have enough confidence to believe that you deserve to be with her. (If you don't believe that, reconsider where you're focusing your efforts. Better to aim a little lower and be secure in yourself than aim too high and spend your life a nervous wreck waiting for your house of cards to fall down on your head when she realizes how much better than you she is. Ideally you both think you got a good deal.)

# DON'T ARGUE

Another way you can ruin things before you ever get to that first date is by arguing with your potential date over stupid shit.

Granted, sometimes two people are so incompatible that an argument is bound to happen, which to me means you really need to just walk away. I mean, honestly, if you can't set up a first date with someone without getting into a disagreement with them? That's not a good sign.

Again, going back to this job interview analogy, would you really argue with your future employer in your job interview? I hope not. Because unless you meet all of their needs and they know there is no one out there even close to comparing to you, you're not going to get that job. They'll move on and find someone more pleasant to work with.

Same with dating. If she has a more pleasant choice and you aren't head and shoulders above her other options, she'll choose him instead.

Don't argue over stupid shit. You have a whole relationship for that.

Here's what happened to me. It's a second date example, but the principle remains the same.

A guy I'd gone out with messaged me about going out again. I said sure and that I was kind of craving brunch, so maybe we could get together on Sunday for brunch somewhere.

Seems simple, right? What's there to argue about there? Well…

He replied that "bunch" sounded like a great idea and then proceeded to suggest a place that didn't actually serve it. When I pointed out to him that the place he'd suggested didn't serve brunch (as I recall it was a very good Mexican place, but definitely not a brunch place), and sent him a link to an article on top brunch places in the area, he argued with me about it by informing me that the place he'd suggested opened at 11.

Problem is, brunch isn't just a meal you have at a certain time of day. It also involves a certain type of food. And guacamole and tacos are not part of that. At least not last time I checked.

So there we were. I had actually been okay with going out with him again (not thrilled and giddy, but okay), but then we got into some ridiculous back and forth about brunch of all things.

If he'd been right about it, I would've conceded the point and maybe, maybe we would've managed to make it to that second date. But he wasn't. And he kept pressing the point and calling it "bunch" and suggesting places that weren't brunch places even though I'd sent him the link with a list of brunch places.

So, instead of going out with him again, I told him I was swamped with work and moved on. And, because he'd lost my interest, that was true. This was a point in my life where I was traveling every single week, Monday through Friday, for work. It didn't take much for me to decide that a man who'd argue with me over "bunch" was not a man who deserved any part of those few precious days I had at home each week.

See, here's the deal. Until you've got someone hooked (think fishing, it's a good analogy), you need to handle them with a bit of care or they'll wriggle free and go about their merry way without you.

And again, going back to the job analogy: Until you've been hired and onboarded and shown that company that you are a rock star that they can't afford to lose, you don't have any sort of job security whatsoever.

You could be the world's greatest and they'll never know if you f it up before you get a chance to show them.

So play nice. Let things slide.

You can be an argumentative asshole later in the relationship when she thinks you're cute and adorable and cranky like an Ewok. At the pre-date stage you pull that shit and she'll just think you're a jerk and move on to the next one.

(And there's *always* a next one…)

# WHERE TO GO ON YOUR FIRST DATE

Alright, so we've resolved that you're not going to be a dumbass between the time she says she'll go out with you and when you actually meet up. Now, what should you *do* for that first date?

My personal opinion is that you shouldn't spend a lot of money. My best first date ever involved cheap beer, a few games of pool, and some late night food at Denny's. It's far more about getting to know each other than being impressed.

(For me. Remember, all women are unique and some will want the fancy schmancy dinner. But don't splash out on a fancy date unless you know that's the kind of woman you're dealing with and you're interested enough to do it. Bottom line here: Don't spend money just because you feel insecure. Okay?)

So, my recommendation is no dinner at Morton's and no hundred-dollar event tickets unless you have season tickets or won them in a contest or something.

Now, the classics these days, especially for someone you've only met online, seem to be meeting for coffee or meeting for a drink. And while there's nothing wrong with those, I kind of hate them.

For two reasons: One, especially with meeting for drinks, it's never really meeting for drinks. It's meeting for a drink so I can determine if you look like your photo and can carry a conversation at which point I suggest we go to dinner somewhere. I hate that. Because I can pass the damned drink test, thank you very much.

But your assumption that I've kept my entire night free so I can pass that little test and we can move on from there?

Eh. I often make plans for dinner with a friend after a drink date because if a guy asked me for a drink, that's what he's getting.

(As I write these books I am continually reminded why I am still single. But just think about it this way: If you can get past someone as obnoxious as me, you'll do fabulous with 90% of women.)

By the way, the way to not annoy me with that sort of thing is to say something like. "Why don't we meet up for a drink and then see where things go from there?"

The other reason I don't like the drink or coffee date is it's so boring and clichéd. Yes, it does give you a chance to talk to someone, so that's a positive. But it also shows a complete lack of originality.

I prefer dates that involve doing something. For example, I've had a couple good first dates where we played pool. It lets you have that drink, but it also involves a fun activity that lets you flirt easily, too.

I also had a decent date where we took our dogs for a walk around a big lake. It let us talk, but also get some exercise in, and, bonus in my book, I didn't have to choose between some guy I didn't know and my dog.

Another good one was meeting up at one of those bars that have old-school video games like Ms. Pac-Man. We got to have our drinks but also played some video games at the same time.

If you do go for an activity date, I'd recommend something that still allows you to interact one-on-one so you can talk and get to know each other. And it should be in a public place.

There are a lot of crazies in this world. Some people don't think about these things, but you really should. For you and for them. Remember, men aren't the only ones who can become obsessive stalkers.

And do something fun or exciting if you can. That little adrenaline rush will get associated with you which is a good thing.

Also, choose a date that shows off your more positive traits or competence. Now is not the time to try to do something for the first time or that you're really bad at. Like bowling or indoor skydiving.

If something came up in your conversations and you can personalize the first date to the woman's interests, do it. A friend of mine and her now-husband had a first date where they went looking for a children's playground because of something they had discussed when they were getting to know each other online.

(That kind of a conversation also makes a nice opening to suggest the date in the first place. You know, "So you love roller coasters? There's a great old one at the amusement park right down the street. We should go check it out sometime.")

I would also recommend that you choose an activity that's an hour or two at most. Half an hour if you're not sure of the person.

And do be flexible about keeping the date going if it's going well. With someone you met in real life that's probably more likely to happen than with someone you met online.

But don't read anything into it if they have to cut the date short or can't extend it. Especially if they have kids or pets. Some people are up against hard deadlines for babysitters or pet sitters.

Chances are, if you haven't met in person, that first date is really just filling in for the conversation you would've had if you'd met at a bar. It's possible you'll meet and click and just keep talking and talking and talking, but it's more likely you'll meet, click, and agree to see each other again soon.

# ONE FINAL NOTE ON COMMUNICATING
# BEFORE THE FIRST DATE

These days I tend to meet men through online dating. And my policy in those situations is to generally avoid giving out my phone number or my email if I can. The site is there to allow us to communicate without getting too much into each other's space, and I think that's a perfectly fine way to reach someone, so that's what I stick to.

I might, on the day of or the day before a date, provide my phone number, or more likely my email, in case something goes wrong and they're running late or can't find me where we're supposed to meet.

But I really don't want the guy to use that to text or call me before the date.

That sounds awful, but fact of the matter is, a guy I've never met in person hasn't earned the right to intrude on my life that much.

I realize some people take a very different approach to this and want to talk on the phone or email or text a lot before they meet up, so all I would say here is to let the woman set the tone and pace. If you ask for her number and she says she doesn't want to provide it yet, don't read anything into that.

She might've just had some creepy experiences like my friend did and has learned from them.

If she does give you her phone number and you send a text or call and she doesn't text you back or call you back, then don't keep trying. And if she takes a long time to respond, then maybe back off.

The slowed response is one of my more subtle ways to slow a guy down. If that doesn't work I often will do the "Wow, you seem to have a lot of time on your hands. Sure you actually have a job?" sort of comment to get a guy to slow it down a bit.

When things are flowing smoothly between you, you'll know it. It's a bit like volleying in tennis. You have to both be engaged in the conversation and willing to go back and forth to keep it going.

I remember on one of the sites I was on there was a chat option, and some guy I was supposed to meet up with a day or two later suddenly sent me a chat message while I was online. Well, that wasn't what I really wanted to be doing. I was on there dealing with messages I'd received from other guys while watching a show I wanted to see (this was pre-DVR days for me), so I was slow to respond and we never really got into a conversational flow since there were a good five minutes between each of my responses.

On the other hand, there was a guy I liked who I would communicate with via Facebook's chat option. The minute he was on there and sent me a hello message we'd start talking back and forth like it was a real in-person conversation. As soon as he finished what he was typing, I'd respond. Or vice versa. We were in synch.

So if you send a text or chat message and you're sitting there for a minute or two straight with no response? That's not a good conversation. Let it go and just focus on getting to that first date, because things can change drastically once you've met in person and really clicked.

# THE FIRST DATE:
# HOW NOT TO SCREW IT UP

Okay. Let's say you survived the landmines of trying to get from "yes" to the actual date.

You're still not in the clear. There are so many things that can go wrong on a first date. Some people approach them with a bunch of hope and optimism, looking to meet "the one." But lots approach them with a certain amount of cynicism looking for those hidden signs that you're a train wreck they need to avoid. (Guess which one I am...)

So this is going to seem like a laundry list of complaints. But it isn't. Just think how you'd feel if someone did these things on your date. Would you really want to go out again with a woman who showed up late, in a crappy outfit that looked like she didn't even try, and then texted with her friends the whole time? No? Well, then don't do that yourself.

The golden rule really does apply here: Do unto others as you'd have them do unto you. Follow that as your guide and nine times out of ten you'll do well.

(The only time that isn't true is when we're talking about the creeper thing. Sadly, I know a number of men who'd love a woman to be overly sexually aggressive with them on a first date. But the reverse is generally not true, so don't do that, not unless she starts it.)

Alright. Let's dive in, shall we?

## Be On Time

Actually, be a little early. Better that than late. You never know what's going to go wrong on the way there so it's always good to build in a bit of a cushion. You really don't want to leave some poor girl sitting around wondering where you are and looking at every guy who walks through the door to see if it's you. That's not a great way to start things off.

And, if you are early, keep an eye out for her so that when she walks in she isn't stuck wondering which of the ten guys sitting alone around the bar are the one she's supposed to meet. It's polite, for starters, and you also don't need her seeing some hot guy at the bar and then seeing you and feeling that little moment of disappointment that she isn't meeting him instead.

(I kid. Sort of.)

## Don't Hang Back Until She Buys Her Drink

I have had this happen at least three times. I've arranged to meet a guy for a drink, arrived, looked around, thought I saw him but wasn't sure, so decided I'd order a drink while I waited for him to arrive. In the meantime, it turned out it was him and he did recognize me and moved closer, but hung back long enough for me to order my drink and pay for it. Only then did he say my name and introduce himself.

Now, clearly, in each instance, the guy recognized me. Two out of three times I was the only woman there. But yet he didn't bother to step in until I'd paid for my own drink.

It didn't end things right then. Two out of three of those, we went on to have dinner and he did pay for dinner. But it was something I noticed and it was a little x in the negative column. And none of the three resulted in a second date.

See, here's why you don't do this. Because by hanging back, you're forcing her to look around the room to find you. (This is also why you should be on time.) And when she has to do that—look at every guy sitting alone long enough to determine if it's you—chances are one of those guys is going to take that as an invitation to come over and say hi.

Think about it. How often do women walk into bars and look around at every single guy long enough for them to notice? Not often and not unless they're looking to be hit on, because that is what will happen.

That's why I order the drink. It buys some time for the guy I'm meeting to recognize me and come over. But just because she started the process of getting a drink doesn't mean you then hang back and let her buy it. As we'll see next, I think the guy should pay for at least the first drink or meal.

## *Pay*

There's a lot of discussion that goes on around this, and I get that. Dating is expensive for men. If you go on twenty dates in a month—which one of my guy friends did when he was single and living in New York City—it can really add up. Especially if you're going through lots of first dates with women that aren't great fits. (May I suggest that you pay less attention to a woman's appearance and more to her personality in the future?)

And it can get tempting to not want to pay. Or to ask to split the dinner tab. But if it's that much of an issue for you, you're better off choosing dates that don't cost money. A walk around a lake, for example. A free concert in the park. A free art exhibit. Whatever.

But if you choose a date that involves spending money, then pay. At least for the first drink or the meal.

Which does not mean the woman should expect you to do so. I always plan on paying for myself, but I'm never impressed when I have to.

Now, someone out there is thinking that in this age of equality, why should a man be the one who pays? And fair enough. I get that it can seem ridiculous. But as equal as men and women are these days, there's still something to be said for the man courting the woman.

And it's not like things are actually equal when it comes to dating. Women are in far more demand than men. With online dating I'd estimate that women probably get twenty or more messages from men for every one message a man gets from a woman. Same with being hit on in person. Men are far more likely to hit on women than women are to hit on men.

So fact of the matter is, you as a man are competing for this woman in a way that she's not competing for you. (At this point. She is competing, too. But it happens earlier in the process. Based on how she dresses and presents herself, men decide whether to hit on her or to hit on someone else. But at the date stage the tables are now turned and she gets to pick from the men who did approach her which ones she wants to keep seeing.)

So at the date stage, impressing your date and standing out from other men is something you should think about.

I don't know other women's pay-to-not-pay ratios, but in my experience it's been about 80% of men will pay and 20% will want to split the check. And I, fortunately, have yet to run into the guy who thinks I should pay or bails on me before the check arrives.

(And if some guy did leave me with the check? As in ordered a bunch of shit and then snuck off to the bathroom after the meal was over and disappeared on me? I'd pay my half and then encourage the restaurant to call the cops on him since he'd run out on his half of it and we hadn't agreed I was paying. And honestly, if a woman did that to a guy—snuck away after ordering a bunch of food—I'd say he had the right to do the same thing.)

Now, I *am* sensitive to these sorts of things, so if a guy I'm on a first date with buys the first round of drinks, I will offer to buy the next round. Or if he buys dinner, I will offer to buy dessert. And I mean it when I make that offer.

But I've learned through painful experience not to insist on doing so.

I had a great first (or maybe second, hard to tell in this

situation) date with a guy that I'd known for a while that involved going dancing at a couple of bars. And, because my guy friends had busted my chops about how guys always have to pay and how unfair it is and how a woman should keep it even, I insisted on buying drinks at the second bar. He didn't want me to, he was fine paying, but I insisted.

After a few hours of salsa dancing we were all comfy cozy when the place closed. But we couldn't leave yet, because I had to close out my tab. Which took some time. And kinda killed the vibe. To this day I wonder how differently things might've gone if I'd just let him buy our drinks that night (he was paying cash).

So the best way I can phrase this is don't fight the flow. Pay if it's easier to do so, let her if it isn't. And don't get hung up on money being spent if there's really something there. Because it'll all even itself out in the end if there is something lasting between you.

## *If You Do Pay, Commit To It*

I should add that if you are going to pay, do so immediately and without hesitation. When the check arrives, I will always reach for my wallet and offer to split it. Nine times out of ten, the guy says, "No, I've got it," and that's it before I can even pull my wallet out of my purse.

But I had one date that was so awkward about paying that he lost all points for doing so.

The check came. I reached for my wallet. I pulled out my wallet. I pulled out my credit card. I reached for the check.

All this time he's talking to me, but making no move towards the check and I'm wondering if he's going to expect me to pay and thinking that's not going to go over well.

Finally, when I put my hands on the check, he reached for it.

Then he took a while to read over it. And I'm sitting there wondering if he's calculating his half (don't do that—if you're going to split the check, just split it 50/50). Finally, he reached for his wallet and said he'd get it.

By letting me think for a good few minutes that he was

going to make me pay or wanted to split it, he lost all goodwill that paying would've earned him. Don't do that.

The best approach is to not even give your date time to reach for her wallet. When the check comes, grab it immediately. If she offers to pay her share (which I would still do and sincerely mean it), tell her you've got it. And then if you need to, only after you've said you've got it, study it to make sure it's accurate. But don't study it before you've confirmed that you're paying.

And don't let her get so far that she's reaching for the check wondering if you even plan to pay your half.

Like I said before, you don't have to pay for her share. There's no requirement. But keep in mind that other men do pay and that's who you're up against. So if you want to split the check you better be bringing more to the table than other guys.

And I'll tell you just anecdotally from my own experience that the men I've gone out with who wanted to split the check were not the ones bringing more to the table. Each one I can think of was a man that I quite frankly wasn't that impressed with before the check arrived, and their wanting to split the check just confirmed things for me.

So do what you want, but don't be penny-wise and pound foolish. Don't lose the girl of your dreams because you wanted to save yourself $25.

Alright, back to some basics.

## *Dress Nice*

You don't need to wear a suit and tie, especially if the occasion doesn't call for it. Jeans and a t-shirt are a perfectly fine choice for a casual date. But make sure that your clothes are clean, and there aren't any holes in them that aren't supposed to be there.

Also make sure your clothes fit you well and are appropriate to the occasion.

Many years ago I met a guy to play pool for a first date. It was not a surprise that we were going to be playing pool because we had very specifically agreed to do so and gone to a pool hall where the only thing to do was play pool.

He happened to wear a pair of jeans that were at least a size too big for him. Which meant that every single shot he took, he had to pull his pants back up afterwards. Now, this wasn't some hip-hop lothario pulling off that sort of gangster look. This was just a normal dude who wore a pair of jeans that didn't fit him well. And every single time he had to pull those pants up, it reminded me that he either hadn't thought much about what we were going to be doing on our date or didn't think much about his appearance or…I don't know.

Whatever the reason, it didn't help. And there wasn't enough about him to overcome the negative impression the poorly-fitting jeans gave.

The goal in dressing nice is to eliminate reasons for the woman to say no to you. You can go one step further and dress well enough to give her a reason to say yes. But, at a minimum, you should dress nice enough to eliminate that as a reason to reject you.

## *Also Don't Wear Anything Offensive*

Now, I've never had this happen, but I could see it being an issue: Do not wear t-shirts or hats that are in some way offensive or off-putting.

A first date is not the time to wear your "making bacon" t-shirt that has two pigs going at it. Not unless you know what kind of woman you're dealing with and are damned sure she'll find it funny. Same with pot-themed clothes. (I'm in Colorado, I have to mention it.) Unless you know she's a pot-smoker herself, you probably don't want to lead with drug use.

And, since this is 2017 and our president is who he is, I wouldn't wear one of those red "Make American Great Again" caps either. That's a good way to find yourself stood up.

## *Don't Be Rude To Others*

Some guys do well at making a woman feel special and well-treated, but then turn around and are absolute assholes to everyone else. They insult the waiter, complain about everyone they know, and are generally jerks to everyone except the person they want something out of—their date.

Some women don't notice this, but I certainly do. And I privately wonder how long he'll be nice to me before he turns on me, too.

A subset of this is the guy who bashes his ex. I talked about this in the online dating books, but let's go over it again: When you talk negatively about your ex—maybe you call her an uptight bitch or say she was too immature for a relationship or use any of a number of other creative and offensive terms to describe her—you're basically telling the woman in front of you that there are circumstances under which a woman you loved and cared for enough to date and possibly marry can go from special and valued by you to whatever nasty terms you're using. Which means *she* can also go from someone you treat with love and respect to someone you hate and bad mouth to strangers.

Now, is it possible that your ex was too immature for a relationship? Sure. Or that she's a crazy psycho? Yeah. But is this date the place to bring that up? No.

If your prior relationship comes up in conversation, the best thing to do is say that it didn't work out. And then move on to some other topic. Focus on the moment and keep the past out of it. There will come a time when you should disclose all of that, but it's not when you're trying to make a good first impression.

(Again, I'm sort of assuming here that this is a woman you don't know already. My mom and my stepdad's first date broke all of the "rules" I'm telling you here, and they've been married over twenty years at this point. But they'd also known each other for a few months before their first date so a lot of that letting someone see that you're not a crazy psycho part of things had already been taken care of.)

## *Don't Talk About Your Ex*

I mentioned already that you shouldn't insult your ex, but really, don't talk about them at all. I can't remember a single time when a guy talked about his ex that it was a good thing for the date.

Examples? Sure, why not.

I had one guy I went out with who was still clearly in love with his ex. He talked about how beautiful she was. He showed me a picture of her. When we dropped by his place he mentioned how she'd decorated it and what a wonderful job she'd done. Eventually, his ex-talk was a big part of why we ended. Because I didn't need to compete with a size two perfect woman who wasn't all the way out of his life.

If he'd instead focused on the moment and me, things would've gone a lot better for us.

Another guy I went on a date with talked about how his ex and he had broken up because she wanted kids, and he wasn't ready for that after five years of dating. He also mentioned that she'd wanted kids the whole time and that he'd never wanted them.

Well, if kids had been a high priority for me in finding someone, that would've ended things right then and there. Because, (a) he didn't want kids and (b) he'd revealed himself to be the kind of guy who would lie to a woman about it to keep her in the relationship. Maybe he'd changed since that relationship, but by talking about that and not giving any other information, he basically put a big red x on himself.

I also had a guy that was actually the opposite of that scenario. He talked about how every woman he dated seemed to want to get serious right away. Spent a good twenty minutes on the topic. Which was a bad thing to do, because when the fact that he had a kid came up and I said I had no interest in being seriously involved with a guy with a kid, although I was fine dating him casually, he freaked out about it. *Even though he'd spent a good twenty minutes talking about women wanting to be too serious.*

So, stay away from the ex talk. It just muddies the waters. Focus on this woman and what you want from her and don't get derailed by talking about other relationships and what you wanted from them. At least not until you hit that "share your soul" point in the relationship.

## Don't Share Too Much

That leads me to add another one. I don't think this is so much a first date issue as a general early relationship issue, but it's worth keeping in mind.

I happen to be a very good listener who will encourage people to talk about whatever it is that's bothering them. I also give good advice and sympathy and support when this happens which makes people comfortable sharing with me things they don't often share with others.

Because of this, I run into a situation that's very challenging, which is that men who don't know me well enough to do so will talk to me about things they never talk to anyone about. Like a brother who was committed to a mental asylum or an ex-girlfriend who was so anorexic she had to be hospitalized or any of a number of other sensitive, personal topics. Things you shouldn't just share if that's not the type of person you are. And especially if the other person isn't being equally candid.

(And who knows maybe I am and don't see it that way because certain life events are so core to who I am that they come up whether someone else would consider that a serious revelation or not.)

While it can feel good to have that conversation, it can create an imbalance of intimacy in the relationship. You feel like you've bared your soul to this person, but they don't know that. For you, this was a huge emotionally weighted event to share this kind of thing. To them it was an emotional conversation that had depth to it, but not something they know they need to protect and handle with care. Not knowing you well enough, they assume that you are always this open which could lead to them mentioning it in a setting or context that feels hurtful to you.

So if you're sharing things that matter to you, make sure the other person is, too. Otherwise, hold back some at that early stage. Yes, true, someone has to go first at opening up, but do it a little bit at a time so you're both moving at the same pace and one of you doesn't get too far ahead of the other.

This section may not have made sense to some of you, and if it didn't, don't worry about it. But hopefully for those who've had this happen, it helped put it in context. As the person on the receiving end of these types of disclosures, let me assure you that any harm that was caused was not caused intentionally.

## *Don't Be Overly Creepy*

By this I mean don't be overly sexual. Just like the emotional intimacy thing where you each need to take small steps towards the other, be sure she's on board with your level of sexual attention.

And it isn't enough that she not react negatively. You need her to be there with you, taking that next step.

What am I talking about?

Example time (again): I was on a first date with a guy who decided towards the end of the night that he should read my palm. It was basically a thinly-veiled excuse to hold my hand and gently stroke my palm with his finger.

Did I yank my hand away from his and tell him to go to hell?

No. I let him do it.

But I also didn't say, "My turn now" and do the same to him. Or let my hand linger in his. Or in any way cross that physical space between us or try to deepen the intimacy of the moment. He did his little hand-holding thing and then I took my hand out of his and drank some beer.

That was not the moment for him to step things up sexually. (But he tried anyway.)

So. How does this work?

You tell an off-color joke and then you see if she responds with one of her own. If she doesn't, you back off.

You let your arm or leg touch hers and you see if she keeps the contact or moves away or maybe even moves closer. If not, you back off.

You bring up some sex-related topic and you see if she just listens to you and changes the subject, or if she adds her own story or comment. If she doesn't add to the conversation, you retreat to something more neutral.

You try, you fail, you retreat.

You try, she matches you, you continue.

Some women will be right there with you. Some will not.

And don't think that because she isn't there in that moment that she isn't interested. She might have some rules about first dates. Or she might have something she needs to work through when it comes to you before she can be comfortable with that. (Like how in love you still are with your ex. Or how much of an ex she actually is.)

You need to give her space to come around, though. Push too hard and you're not getting that chance.

(And, by the way, it's okay for you to decide that you'd rather date the kind of woman who is right there with you from day one. If you think this woman is standoffish or prude or rude or whatever, you don't have to ask her out again. *Even if she's attractive.* I assume the reason you care about her looks is because you want something to happen with her? But if she's not really on the same page with you when it comes to that, it's probably not going to go well when it does happen.)

## Leave Your Phone Alone

Let's drop back to a basic one. If you're on a date with a woman, be focused on her. That means no pausing every ten seconds to respond to texts and no taking phone calls unless they're unexpected ones you think might be important.

(I once got a call from my grandma in the middle of a date

to tell me my mom was in the hospital. I didn't take the actual call, but did check the message since my grandma normally doesn't leave them.)

And stay off the internet, too. If your date goes to the bathroom, fine. Entertain yourself. But if she's sitting right there in front of you? Focus on her.

And expect her to do the same for you.

(Or I guess you could both be on your phones the whole time in which case you're well-matched, but ugh. Who wants that? What kind of a relationship is it where you're both more interested in other events and people than spending time with one another?)

## Don't Flirt With Others

This should be obvious, but don't hit on other women while you're on a date with this one.

You think it doesn't happen, but it does. When I was young and foolish I dated a guy who was every sort of wrong for me. And he really was the world's biggest, most ridiculous flirt. Got us free food at McDonald's one time, but it was completely inappropriate and I never put up with that shit from a guy again.

If you want to be a charming, flirtatious guy that every woman loves, be one. Just do it when you're alone. Not with your date sitting right there.

Now, some guys are just charming. It's like it oozes from their pores. That's fine. Although you'd be better off turning that charm on your date.

But asking some other woman if she has a boyfriend or telling her she's attractive or asking when she gets off or what her number is? No. That's too much.

## Don't Insult Her

We touched on this a bit when I mentioned that arguing with a potential date isn't going to help get you to the actual date, but there's another one in here to consider, which is that it's never a good idea to criticize or insult your date.

When I told a friend of mine that I was writing this book and asked her for some of her horror stories—and she has a lot because she was much more open-minded about meeting up with her potential matches than I ever was—the first guy she thought of was the one who said, "You must've been hungry" when she finished eating her dinner.

Never comment on what a woman eats, whether it's too much or too little.

Our society has too many issues with women and food and weight, and a seemingly innocuous comment can actually be loaded with all sorts of judgmental bullshit most women aren't going to want to hear.

You want to ask if her food tastes good? Okay. You want a bite? Fine. You want to offer her a bite of yours? Fine. But don't comment on the type or quantity she just ate or didn't eat. Ever.

(There's a school of thought that some men follow that argues that insulting a woman is a good way to get her attention. It's included in a whole slew of dating books about unlocking the secrets to women and how to get any woman. My thoughts? Don't do it. Because for every woman that sort of thing works on, there's another who will never give you the time of day again. And, honestly, most men don't know the difference between being insulting and busting someone's chops a bit. You insult a woman, you're done. You playfully poke at her ego, you might be fine. But can you really tell the difference? Probably not. So best to not risk falling on the wrong side of that line.)

## Compliment Her But Not Too Much

Should you compliment your date? Yeah, sure. It can help. A simple, "You look lovely this evening," never goes wrong.

Just be careful that your compliments don't turn to gushing. Remember that whole, you're her equal and you need to act it thing? Keep that in mind.

I've had guys go overboard on the compliments. Like they couldn't stop once they started. I've also had them compliment me but in a "oh, I didn't realize you were that far out of my league" sort of way.

(Typing that makes me sound so damned arrogant. But it really has happened. Like they knew I was smart, but they didn't realize I was that smart.)

So, anyway. One sincere, honest compliment and then you're done for the night.

Of course, as with all of my advice, take into account what type of woman this is and what she's indicated she likes or wants from men. I clearly don't like being put on a pedestal, but some women will eat that shit up. You need to know which you're dealing with and act accordingly.

# SIDE NOTE:
## WOMEN ARE INDIVIDUALS

I've mentioned this a few times, but let's go over it again. Because it really is central to you being successful at dating.

Women are individuals.

What works for one may not work for another.

You're probably thinking, well, duh. Of course women are individuals, aren't we all?

But when you're reading a book on how to approach a large group of people, be it women or co-workers or the general public, this can tend to get lost. And what ends up happening is you get told that X approach works all the time.

But, honestly, that's not true. I for one do not like getting flowers. And yet if you watch commercials in February of every year you'd walk away convinced that the way to show affection or interest to a woman is to give her a bunch of red roses. Or chocolate. Or a stuffed animal.

(For the record, two of the best gifts guys ever gave me were stuffed animals. But not just any stuffed animal. In both cases the guy gave me a stuffed animal customized to me in some special way. One was an inside joke, one matched the colors of my apartment perfectly.)

Now, giving flowers can be a sort of cultural shortcut. We all know that red roses mean romantic interest so if you give them you're telling her that you are romantically interested.

But it's so generic. And there's no acknowledgement there that the woman is an individual who needs to be treated as unique.

You're far better off thinking about the specific woman you're dealing with and actually interacting with her on an individual basis.

Basically: Listen to what she says and respond to that. Don't base your actions or decisions on what you think women as a whole want or will do.

Like this book. I just told you all sorts of things not to do on a first date. And yet, if you talk to a bunch of happy couples you'll find that they violated one or more of these.

Maybe they slept with the person on the first date. Or stayed up until four in the morning talking about everything in their lives, including all of their exes and every deep intimate secret they'd never told anyone else.

Or maybe she was three hours late but he waited for her and it's now their favorite little story to tell.

So, while you should keep in mind these "rules", feel free to call an audible if it makes sense in the moment.

(Although, if you're really bad at reading women's cues, I'd suggest you don't actually try that. At least follow these rules until you're at date three or four.)

# IT'S OKAY TO NOT WANT TO
# GO OUT AGAIN

If you've been single long enough you've probably been told (at least I and most of my female friends have) that you should give someone a try. Go out on a few dates before you write them off. Don't be so picky.

Or, maybe this is more the scenario for men, you meet a woman who is so attractive that you can't think about anything else. Including the fact that she's awful for you.

So you keep going on dates with her even though it makes you miserable. Maybe you think once you sleep together it'll get better. (It won't. You'll just stay with her that much longer because, hey, sex.)

Don't do that to yourself. It's okay to go on one date and decide this person isn't the one for you.

And I'm not saying that just because I'm an insanely picky judgmental person who rarely changes my mind and has yet to give someone a second chance and be glad I did.

Most of my friends who are happily married or in good relationships felt a click with their significant other the first time they met them. They may not have dated them right away, because the person was in a relationship or a co-worker or whatever, but they did feel that little spark of interest.

It wasn't just physical attraction either. It was something more.

So if you're on a date and you don't feel anything positive about seeing this person again, move on. Because every moment you spend with this person who isn't right for you is a moment that you aren't spending on finding the right person for you.

I think too often people get scared or worried that they'll be alone and they settle for "good enough." But it isn't. That person you're settling for is someone else's dream partner. So let them go find that person who will adore them, and you find that person you'll adore and who'll adore you.

# THE THIRD DATE ISSUE

While we're talking, let me tell you about the third date issue I see with too too many men.

On a first date I'm generally vetting a guy to see if we're compatible. So I'm listening to how he approaches the world and looking for any red flags that we won't work long-term. How does he talk about other people? Does he like his life? If not, is he doing anything to change it? Is he smart? Is he nice? Is he funny?

Basically, do I like this guy?

Unfortunately, most men aren't really listening to a thing I say.

I could tell them I engage in voodoo and cut the heads off chickens and they'd just shrug and smile and keep going. I call it the third-date problem. Because I swear that until we get past the third date the only thing on a guy's mind is whether he thinks he can sleep with me or not.

Only after we get past that point does he suddenly seem to realize that we have all sorts of differences that aren't going to work for him.

Now, granted, this is a broad generalization and not all men are that way. But you'd be surprised how many first dates I've been on where it was abundantly clear to me that we were not compatible at all and the guy didn't seem to notice.

I've even pointed these things out to some of the guys. Like, "Hey, you are devoutly religious and want to raise your children in your faith and I am not willing to do that." And they say something like, "Oh, you'll come around." Or "Oh, we'll work through it."

No we won't.

But because the guy is so caught up on the physical side of things he doesn't see the rest of it.

That puts all of the heavy lifting of judging the relationship's potential on me. And, yes, there are people who will happily sleep with someone they don't necessarily like and be fine with it, but I'm not that person. So it's a waste of a guy's time to ignore the non-physical for the physical.

So all I'm saying is maybe try to step back a bit and focus less on how attractive your date is and more on whether the two of you could stand to be stuck in an elevator together for four hours straight.

If you couldn't, then walk away.

Looks are not everything.

I know, sacrilege. But seriously? If you're in this for the long-term, remember that people get old. They get wrinkles and cellulite and serious illnesses and things that you don't want sagging start to sag. Badly. If you want a relationship that will last the rest of your life, you need to like this person enough and they need to like you enough that none of that matters.

Think about it.

But I digress.

# WRAPPING UP THE FIRST DATE

So you had a first date. It went well. Time for it to end. What do you do so you can see this woman again?

If it was a really fabulous date, you don't have to do much. Because you probably already geeked out together over something you both like and you already have a specific thing you want to do together. Like, "Oh my god, I've been dying to go to that new sushi place, too," sort of thing.

In that case, when it comes time to wrap things up, you say, "So what do you think? You want to go to that sushi place on Thursday?"

And she says, "Absolutely." Or, "Oh, I have plans on Thursday, but what about Sunday?"

And you make a *specific* plan to get together to do a *specific* thing at a *specific* time.

If you didn't have that fabulous a date, that doesn't mean all hope is lost. You can still do the standard, "I had a good time. You want to get together again?" and she will say, "Sure, I'd like that." And then you will call her and set something up later.

But keep this in mind—especially if it was a never-met-before date—until you have firm plans set, you really don't know if you're going to get a second date or not.

We're back into the "yeah, sure" stage of things. The "it's easier for me to say yes than to reject him to his face" stage.

And if you press to make firm plans and she's not quite sure she wants to really see you again, she's gonna sidestep that question and say something like, "I really can't commit to anything right now. Work's gonna be insane this week and I need to see what my boss is going to throw at me before I know if I'll have any free time."

She likely won't tell you right there to your face that she doesn't want to see you again.

So how can you tell if you've got a shot?

Well, do you have her phone number? Or email?

Or are you still relying on the dating site you used to meet her?

If you end the first date without getting direct contact information for this woman, no matter how well it feels like it went, chances are you're not going to see her again.

Because all she has to do is say, "yeah, sure," and then go home and close down the match. So, if you can, be sure to ask for her number or email if you don't already have it. If she hesitates to give it to you at this stage, you're very likely not going to see her again.

But she won't tell you that, she'll just tell you to reach out through the site because it's easier that way.

# WHAT YOU SHOULD NEVER DO:
## A CASE STUDY

I've definitely had guys I would've probably gone out with again who dropped the ball in one way or another and never tried again. Like the guy who was a friend of a friend and asked about going out but didn't get my number and made no effort to follow up with our mutual friend.

There was another guy who I'd met online dating who said he'd reach out to me and didn't and I think it was because he got home and thought it was my turn to message him on the site and didn't realize he could message me, and I wasn't quite interested enough to reach out to him. (Of course, maybe he got home and thought "eh, not interested" but I'm a pretty good judge of a guy's interest and I think he was interested enough that that's not what happened.)

So, to a certain extent, I would encourage guys to try a little extra after a first date if they really like a woman and haven't been told "no" directly.

(Although, know that in most instances you're wasting your time pursuing her further.)

(And if she is the type of woman who *deliberately* tries to make it hard for you so she can know you're really interested, think about whether that's what you want in your life. No matter how attractive a woman is, she should treat you with decency.)

What you should not do, under any circumstances, is what this guy did to my friend.

A bit of background: They went on two dates. She probably should've called it after one date, but my friend is nice and was very serious about meeting someone so she went on date number two. Just in case. After that second date she told him straight up in an email that she wasn't interested in seeing him again.

What did he do next?

He called her.

When she didn't take his call, he sent her an email acknowledging that his continued pursuit of her might be pushing her even further away or seen as desperate. He then proceeded to write a number of lengthy paragraphs about why *he* liked *her* so much.

When that didn't work he showed up at her office with flowers.

No.

No.

No.

Do not do this. For every one woman that is won over by your ardent interest and inability to give up on her, there will be eight that send your heartfelt email to their friends with an "OMG" comment, and one who calls the cops to see if she can get a restraining order. (I suspect you know by now which one I would be.)

What is so wrong with what this guy did?

First, never, ever show up at a woman's work after she's rejected you. You may think it makes perfect sense because you know she'll be there and all you want to do is talk and you know you can find her there.

She thinks (or maybe this is just me) about all those crazy stalker types who've killed their ex-wives or ex-girlfriends by showing up at their work brandishing a weapon and demanding that she talk to them.

(As I write this, the news coverage has a story about a man who did this at an elementary school and ended up killing his wife, himself, and an eight-year-old child. No matter what week I chose to write this, there would be a story like that on the news. Yes, women can do this crazy shit, too. And women have killed their partners. But it is far more likely that a man will kill his partner.)

So some guy a woman rejected showing up at her work unasked for is a HUGE red flag. HUGE.

DO NOT DO THIS. EVER.

EVER. EVER. EVER.

She said no. Move on.

But if you can't bring yourself to let go of this perfect woman that easily, then you need to make your case from a distance and you need to focus on what she overlooked about you.

You do not write to her to tell her how beautiful she is and how much *you* want *her*. She knows that. Chances are, if she's decent looking, this is not the first time in her life that a man found her attractive but she wasn't interested in him. Your interest in her is irrelevant.

You need *her* to be interested in *you*.

So if you want to win her over, you need to tell her what it is about you that you somehow failed to convey in the dates you went on that she would want.

Or you clarify the misunderstanding you guys had that led to her deciding she didn't want to see you again. (For example, "I'm sorry about that scene at the restaurant. That was my sister playing a joke on me, but you didn't stick around long enough for her to tell you that.")

Often in these cases a man keeps reaching out because he wants the woman and he thinks for some reason the degree to which he wants her should convince her to want him back.

That's not how it works.

(And if you are someone who thinks like that? If you've done something like this in the past? Been so in love with a woman that you couldn't let go or see why she didn't want you back? You need to sit down with a professional to work through why you did it and how not to do it again.)

# HOW TO OVERCOME AN INITIAL REJECTION

So what *do* you do if you really liked a woman and she told you straight-up that she's not interested in seeing you again. Or if she ghosted you or shut down your online match after the date?

My personal recommendation is to move on. Chalk it up to not everyone is compatible and what you think you see or feel is not what the other person is seeing or feeling.

Nine times out of ten she knows her own mind and you trying to convince her to give you another chance isn't going to work. It'll just be awkward for both of you.

If she shut down the match or told you no—so took a direct action to not see you again—the chances of bringing her around are about one in a hundred. If that.

But sometimes things do fall through the cracks.

I had a guy email me a while back and his email ended up in my spam filter. I did see it, but many women wouldn't have. And he'd be sitting there thinking, "Oh, she doesn't want to see me," when what really happened is she never even knew he reached out.

So, this is what you can do if you really must:

If you called her and left a message and didn't get a response, you can send her a quick email that says, "Hey, tried to call you. Don't know if you got the message. Call or write back at XXX-XXXX. I'd love to see you again."

If you emailed her and got no response, you can drop her a quick text. "Sent you an email. Was hoping to get together again. Reach out if you're interested."

Something like that. It's short and to the point and the assumption here is that she didn't get your first communication. It's the only reason you should be reaching out to her—if you think she somehow didn't get that first message.

What do you do if you only have one way of reaching her? A way that clearly didn't work the first time around.

You can see if there's an easy second way to reach her. Say you have mutual friends on Facebook. You could reach out to her that way. But even as I type this I'm thinking "no, no, no." Same with LinkedIn or Twitter or finding her business email.

It's all just...too stalkery.

Now, full disclosure here. I have in the past (a) dropped by the work of a guy who casually said we should go out some time to ask him when that was going to happen and (b) messaged some guy I'd met and liked after tracking him down on Facebook.

In both cases I was "successful" at reviving something that I had no other way to move forward because I didn't have their phone numbers or emails. (In hindsight, both were a bad idea. But it did work. And we did go out or stay in touch after I did it.)

But, I'm a woman. And the rules, like it or not, are different for women.

Or, and this is even worse, the rules are different for someone you find attractive.

If I sat next to some really good-looking guy on a plane flight and we had a great conversation but then didn't exchange numbers and he tracked me down via my LinkedIn, I'd probably be more flattered than disturbed.

But if I had a lengthy conversation with some guy on a plane flight who wasn't attractive to me and he did the same thing, I'd probably be a little creeped out.

And in this case, we're talking about a situation where you already had a date. You had your chance to reel her in and you blew it somehow.

So, really? Best to move on. Your level of interest likely does not match hers.

Plenty of fish in the sea. If it was meant to be you'll cross paths again. Yada, yada, yada.

# AFTER THE FIRST DATE: KEEP PLAYING IT COOL

So what about if you did ask her out for a second date and she said yes. Now what?

Now we move into the "everyone is different" stage of dating. Where how you act and behave is dictated by the person you're dating.

Seriously, after that first date, it's all about the two individuals and how they move forward together. But I will tell you that I've had a good first date with a guy and then decided I really didn't want to see him again because of how he acted before the second date.

I already mentioned one of the examples above where the guy called brunch "bunch" and then argued with me about what it was.

Another was a guy who became way too serious way too fast. I honestly think wedding bells were going off in his head after that first date. He started sending me virtual roses and being far too aggressive about how much he liked me.

Some women will eat that up. The more the better. And maybe if he'd been a different guy, I would've eaten it up, too. But I wasn't as interested as he was, so all it did was scare me off.

So, after the first date, no matter how you're feeling and even if she said yes to another one and is responding to your messages, pay attention to how often she responds and what she says.

Does she take your phone calls or just text or email or message? If so, how long do you guys stay on the phone when you talk? Is she flirty? Is she all business? If you send a text, does she respond right away? Or wait for a day?

Whatever she does, mirror her. If she's all about the details of the second date and not interested in talking or communicating back and forth, then be that way, too. Don't send five messages for every one she sends you.

(And again, as a woman, I can think of situations where I did these things I'm telling you not to do and it worked, but...don't do it. It never ends well. You want a balance with this other person so you're moving forward at the same pace. It's too easy to get too far ahead of them and then have it fall apart, or find that you feel very different things from what they feel.)

But it's also okay to move fast *as long as she is, too.*

My friend who is happily married and expecting her first child moved in with her now-husband within a couple of weeks of their first date. And they were married eight months later. So things can move fast. But both people have to be on board with it. You can't just really like someone and make it happen on your own. That's a good way to lose them instead.

# JUST FOR KICKS: MY REASONS FOR NOT WANTING TO SEE A GUY AGAIN

This is not a list you should use as any sort of resource. This is more a list that shows that sometimes it's not about you. Or it is about you but not in any way you can fix. Some matches just don't work and that's part of dating and something you need to understand so you can move forward and find the woman who is right for you.

Also, note that some of these were for the same person, so in isolation they weren't a reason to reject a guy but when combined with a few others they were.

Ready? Reasons I didn't want to go out with a guy again:

1.  He liked cats and had one at home. (I'm allergic and hate them.)

2.  He had a long-term illness that was going to impact his quality of life. (Been there, done that, didn't want to do it again.)

3.  He showed signs of anger issues. (I have zero tolerance for men with tempers.)

4.  At first I thought he was a gracious loser and then I realized he was just really used to losing at things. (As someone who is fiercely competitive, this was a turn off.)

5. He was overly aggressive sexually and not attractive enough to me for that to work.

6. He had a kid.

7. He had no ambition.

8. We talked about accounting for the entire date. (I can talk about anything with anyone for an hour, but that doesn't mean I want to repeat that experience ever again.)

9. He called himself a foodie but we went to a chain Italian restaurant for the date.

10. He wanted to split the check. (This only comes into play when combined with others on the list.)

11. He was incredibly awkward to talk to. There was no flow to our conversation.

12. It felt more like a job interview than a date. He asked rapid-fire questions about where I wanted to be in five years.

13. He wanted marriage and kids NOW.

14. He seemed a bit intimidated by what he learned about me and I'd been holding back a number of things.

15. We had absolutely nothing in common.

16. I didn't find him attractive. (Looks are only part of this for me. A really interesting personality can partially compensate for not being classically good-looking.)

17. He talked down about others a lot.

18. He was too focused on status and one-upping others.

19. Our attitudes towards money were completely incompatible.

20. Our backgrounds were too different for me to ever be comfortable with him.

21. He was too nice. (I knew the first time I was in a bad mood I'd tear him to shreds.)

22. He referred to women who wear a size large at Victoria's Secret as fat. (Even while eyeing me up and down like some prize piece of meat.)

23. He was too focused on his career or hobbies or other interests to actually have room for me in his life.

24. He told me stories that showed he would cut corners or break rules at work or in his career if it let him get ahead temporarily.

25. He wasn't smart.

26. He was offensive.

27. He said he hated living in my home state and wanted to leave as soon as possible.

28. He wasn't close to his family.

29. He didn't like dogs.

30. He was very religious.

31. He was very anti-religion.

32. He clearly wasn't interested in a committed relationship.

33. His appearance was sloppy.

34. He had a go-nowhere job and no apparent ambition.

35. He had failed at things I thought should be easy. In other words, I didn't respect him.

# CONCLUSION

So there you have it. Let's see if we can sum up.

- Until you actually make it to the first date, you aren't guaranteed that that date will happen.

- Especially if you met the woman in person, she may not have had any intent of ever seeing you again.

- Even if she did think she wanted to meet up with you, you can turn that yes into a no by saying something rude or getting too comfortable too soon or making her realize she's out of your league or failing to manage the negotiation of where to go and what to do effectively.

- The first date can also be fraught with opportunities to blow things and lose the girl.

- You want to be on time, pay for her drink or meal without making a big deal out of it, dress nicely, and focus on her.

- On a date you shouldn't be rude to other people, talk about your ex, overshare, get too sexual if she isn't onboard with it, flirt with others, insult her, or spend too much time on your phone.

- All of this goes out the window depending on the woman you're dealing with and your best bet to dating success is to pay attention to her and what she wants.

- You should have some pride in yourself and insist that a woman treat you right as well.

- Even if a woman is attractive, that doesn't mean you need to put up with poor treatment. Instead, move on to find a woman who will treat you well.

- Men can sometimes get a little too hung up on the physical side of things early on and you'd be much better off if you stepped back and made sure there was actually something there between you other than your physical attraction to her.

- If a woman does turn you down, best to just move on.

- If you can't bring yourself to move on, then try one simple, basic attempt to show her why you are worth giving another chance (and it can't be because you really like her), and then move on.

- Under no circumstance should you ever show up at the workplace of a woman who rejected you.

- There are any number of reasons a woman might not want to see you again that have nothing to do with you and everything to do with her, so don't get hung up on it. Just move on to someone who will like you for who you are.

Bottom line is to try to make the best impression you can until you're about three dates in or she's so obviously infatuated with you that you're on the right track. But accept that not all dates will work out either and move on from those that don't so you can focus on the ones that will. And applying the golden rule of treating others how you'd like to be treated is going to overcome many of the reasons a first date doesn't succeed.

I know the whole process can be a frustrating nightmare.

But I also have any number of friends who've persevered and found someone who truly made their lives better, so don't give up. Remember what you want out of a relationship and insist on getting that. Don't settle because you're tired or desperate. It'll happen. You just have to push through.

Good luck!

# ABOUT THE AUTHOR

Cassie Leigh is a bit like that Catholic nun that used to slap your hand with a ruler when you did something wrong. Is she sweet and gentle? No. Is she effective? Yes.

She's a woman who's been there, done that, and has a few opinions as a result. And, in her own not at all humble opinion, you'd do well to listen to her.

You can reach her at cassieleighauthor@gmail.com.

www.ingramcontent.com/pod-product-compliance
Lightning Source LLC
Chambersburg PA
CBHW051714020426
42333CB00014B/980